WARRIOR PARENT
PLAYBOOK

WARRIOR PARENT
PLAYBOOK

UTILIZING SPORTS TO EMPOWER CHILDREN
TO LIVE IN GREATNESS

JAVELIN M. GUIDRY

ISBN 978-1-7359314-0-1
ISBN 978-1-7359314-1-8 eBook

Cover and interior design by Peter Gloege

Printed in the United States of America
20 21 22 23 24 25 26 27 28   (ING)   10 9 8 7 6 5 4 3 2 1

For my dad, Edward "Ace" Guidry
Thanks, Dad, for showing me what a
Warrior Parent looks like.
The Guidry Legacy lives on...

Thank you to my amazing wife, Kaishauna
"Dr. MamaKai" Guidry, physician and co-Warrior Parent,
I love you! We Are One!

Thank you to my three awesome children,
Javelin KaJireh, Elisha JaNoah, and Kailah Grace.
You inspire and bring the best out of me
I love you! Show the world YOUR greatness!

CONTENTS

FOREWORD

By Roderick L. Hairston, M.A.

ONCE IN A WHILE, someone emerges from obscurity
with insights, counsel, and perspective that can launch a much-
needed revolution in some area of human experience. Author
Javelin M. Guidry (along with his wife, Kaishauna Guidry MD,)
has done just that. *Warrior Parent Playbook* is a long-awaited
resource, bringing inspiration, guidance, hope, and clarity to
parenting as it reveals the powerful tool that sports can be in
a parent's hands.

As the tutor, so popular in the Roman Empire, shaped
the hearts and minds of Rome's next generation, youth sports
share similar potential. And this time, parents get to lead the
way rather than pass the responsibility on to a special class of
instructors and institutions.

Parents, this is your book! No one can inspire and help
release the greatness that resides in your children like you. *Warrior Parent Playbook* equips you to partner with the ubiquitous
industry of sports to shape, inspire, teach, and champion your

child's greatness, using the pillars of love, discipline, and emotional and relational acuity. More than an instruction manual on making kids behave, *Warrior Parent Playbook* provides clarifying insights about more important matters. It will help you assess motives, see the best in your kids, and come alongside them as a parent-coach!

I have worked for more than 30 years as a chaplain in NCAA Division I sports, and I have served as an NFL "life coach," earning two Super Bowl rings in the process. I know the power of sports. I've seen firsthand the damage sports can do when parents determine children's worth by their performance. So many young athletes become unsure of themselves, no matter how talented they are. They struggle with their self-esteem, with depression and anxiety, often resorting to various addictions. They scream out loud for someone to love them and accept them.

Fortunately, when parents partner with the game and use sports as a tool for development, kids become productive in whatever career path they choose. More important, they become champions for the good of others.

Clearly, this book is onto something: the potential to help America recover the value of good families, connected communities, workplace integrity, and sane governance. Today's child is tomorrow's leader. Family is still the foundation of society.

As the family goes, so goes the nation. May *Warrior Parent Playbook* be a source of hope, clarity, and inspiration for you. May it equip you as you seek to draw out the genius and greatness so beautifully planted in your kids. Someday, they will rise up and joyfully call you blessed for utilizing sports to effectively launch them as arrows into a world that needs them!

—Roderick L. Hairston, M.A.

Pastor, Author, Speaker, Marriage Coach,
and two-time Super Bowl Champion

INTRODUCTION

SPORTS: A TRANSFORMATIONAL LIFE PLATFORM

IN 2018, the global sports market reached a value of $488.5 billion (according to Businesswire, a Berkshire Hathaway company). That's a current market value greater than 8 out of the top 10 Fortune 500 Companies.[1] However, while its economic value is higher than industry giants like Walmart, AT&T, Exxon Mobile, United Health, and others, sport's true value is realized in the life transformation and inspiration it brings to millions of people, especially our youth.

According to the Aspen Institute, young athletes enjoy a variety of benefits that improve their lives in myriad ways. Active kids score up to 40-percent higher on academic tests. They are 15-percent more likely to attend college than their non-active counterparts. They are less likely to smoke, use drugs, or participate in risky sex. They experience lower rates of depression and obesity. They earn more in their careers, and that's only the beginning.[2]

Competitive sports mirror so many lessons and challenges that everyday young people will face, both now and as they enter adulthood. I am biased, but I believe that competitive sports teach and prepare young people for life better than any other institution. However, these benefits will be realized only if young people develop and learn to use those acquired life skills, skills which are honed during hundreds and hundreds of hours, season after season.

Let's compare sports to a school's academic curricula. For example, a high school English class is group-oriented, as is the high school football team. Both involve learning and reaching goals and in a group-oriented, problem-solving learning environment.

A coach creates a game plan. A teacher creates a lesson plan. A teacher makes corrections on tests and in class discussions. This teacher might give the class a break during a difficult assignment, or a long test. A coach calls time-out to give the team a rest or to help settle down the players, if needed. A coach makes corrections in practice, and, often, during the course of a game.

Students get report cards, while athletes are often given "game grades," evaluating both individual and team performance. Coaches and teachers measure success by grades, points, and other relevant statistical measures. Good coaches and teachers strive to give kids a positive and rewarding experience. Relationships are developed, and personal growth is achieved.

However, with sports, kids also get free snacks and drinks every week. Who wouldn't want their children to sign up for that experience?

Seriously though, sports have the potential to cultivate total personal development: mentally, socially, emotionally, and physically. This kind of development has lifelong implications and provides building blocks for success in pursuit of any ambition. If a kid falls in love with sports, he or she will enjoy a variety of career opportunities—beyond being a professional athlete. Today's job market provides opportunities in sports medicine, sports media, sports management, sports marketing, personal training, coaching, and administration.

Competitive sports offer a setting like no other. You learn to truly appreciate a sport, its history, its complexities, and its role models. And you develop physical and mental skills and learn important life lessons.

> Sports have the potential to cultivate total personal development: mentally, socially, emotionally, and physically. This kind of development has lifelong implications and provides building blocks for success in pursuit of any ambition.

Little League Baseball,[3] for example, provides a team environment that is both competitive and cooperative. There are clear obstacles, like the opposing pitcher, or the way the infield and outfield shift, depending on who is at bat. And there are unpredictable circumstances, like the weather or a star player missing a game due to illness or injury. The game requires young athletes to rise up and face challenges, over and over again.

In short, sports prepare kids for life, but in a relatively safe and controlled environment.

This book would be too long if I listed all of the advantages of sports, but I will highlight 4 key life skills that sports help kids develop:

SOCIAL DEVELOPMENT

» Relationship skills. Children learn to work with others toward a goal, and to develop new friendships.

» Verbal and nonverbal communication skills are cultivated.

» Young athletes learn to be "coachable." In other words, they take instruction and correction. They learn to process information and apply it immediately.

» They learn to respect authority as they interact with coaches, referees, scorekeepers, adult volunteers, and so on.

EMOTIONAL DEVELOPMENT

» Sports encourage enjoying the athletic experience and loving the game. Kids are taught to enjoy what they are doing.

›› Young athletes learn to overcome the fear of failure as they learn from their mistakes and keep on trying. They learn that weaknesses can be overcome through practice, patience, and perseverance.

›› They learn to overcome losses. They learn and grow from them, rather than becoming discouraged or wallowing in misery.

›› Sports teach poise and the ability to perform in high-pressure situations.

MENTAL DEVELOPMENT

›› Sports create ample opportunities to develop problem-solving skills, both individually and as a team.

›› Sports build critical-thinking skills during practices and games. A young athlete learns how to analyze opponents, situations, and various game plans and strategies, both their own and those of the opposing team.

›› Young athletes learn to compete and practice with purpose and *passion.*

›› Mental toughness and grit are forged through overcoming difficulties in practices and games, as well as the occasional bumps, bruises, and other injuries.

›› Sports also develop "intangible" skills like creativity, resilience, empathy, humility, imagination, and more.

PHYSICAL DEVELOPMENT

» Youth sports teach the value of exercise and nutrition, which every parent and coach hopes will become a lifestyle.

» Sports strengthen bones, joints, and muscles, especially the brain and heart muscles!

» Young athletes enjoy an increased level of energy, and a high level of conditioning that helps them with a variety of everyday tasks and responsibilities.

» Beyond all the benefits listed above, sports also reduce the risk of disease, obesity, depression, and anxiety.[4]

I hope the list above broadens your perspective on sports—and piques your curiosity to learn more about how you can optimize the value your child can experience from the sports that millions of people enjoy every day. Regardless of your child's athletic ability, I believe this playbook will provide treasures of information, practical wisdom, and valuable experiences that will help propel him or her to live a championship life. No matter your knowledge level or interest in sports, this playbook will speak to your role as a parent and empower you to take intentional action to help your child live in their greatness.

SECTION ONE

SPORTS AND TOTAL PERSONAL DEVELOPMENT

1

A CHAMPIONSHIP LIFE!

(THE DREAM IS THE JOURNEY, NOT THE DESTINATION.)

"It is good to have an end to journey towards;
but it is the journey that matters, in the end."

—URSULA K. LE GUIN[1]

IN 2019, Los Angeles Lakers five-time NBA champion Kobe Bryant concluded his 20-year basketball career retirement speech (as the whole world watched), with a message not as an elite basketball player but as a dad to his daughters. He noted, "The dream is not the destination, but the journey." He spoke of his legacy as a father, sharing what he learned through all the hard work and dedication to basketball. I believe he was speaking to all us who dream of a championship life, to all who aspire to enjoy the journey and embrace each stage of life as we experience it.

At the core of every parent's desire for their child is for them to have a rich and fulfilling life. A life even better than their dreams. We want the best possible lives for our kids, and that desire originates from a heart of pure and enduring love. Remember when you looked into those young eyes for the first time? Do you recall the joy, the euphoria, and (perhaps) a little fear—fear that now you are responsible for this new living being who longs for your love and depends on you completely?

As a new parent, you have the opportunity and the power to shape and directly impact the trajectory of your child's life for the next 18 or 19 years, if not more. However, (as Uncle Ben told Peter Parker, aka Spider-Man): "With great power comes great responsibility." [2]

What does that phrase mean for us parents? Is it working hard to give kids the best material things and the most-wonderful experiences? Is it emulating our own parents—or doing everything the opposite of how we were raised? There is no perfect science or predictive analytics to help drive every parenting decision. However, one thing is clear at your child's birth: You've signed this "player" to your team, with an 18-year, fully guaranteed in-house contract. There's no trade clause,

> "Success is a journey, not a destination. The doing is often more important than the outcome."
>
> —ARTHUR ASHE [3]

and this contract is binding, per the birth certificate and DNA records (or the adoption papers). So, we need to develop a parent playbook that can help us toward a championship life.

In sports, a coach creates a playbook or game plan by spending hours studying and researching the game; understanding the players' capabilities, strengths, and weaknesses (and those of the opponents); considering a variety of game scenarios; and so much more. As a coach, you must figure out what works for your team as you try to create the best conditions for success. Similarly, I've created this parent playbook, designed to produce two key outcomes that almost every parent will endorse:

1. Develop life skills for success now, and into the future.
2. Empower your child to live in his or her *greatness*.

Remember, a sports playbook is not designed to earn the team a participation trophy. A playbook embodies the vision, the mission for the season. For most of us, that mission includes developing key skills and teamwork, and, yes, winning games. In life, like sports, there is a difference between existing (going through the motions) and living with purpose (playing with passion). I want to be clear; we are seeking the latter.

I firmly believe that sports provide a platform filled with life lessons that can develop and empower young people to win in life, to live a life filled with significance. Sports involve triumphs, defeats, adversity, working together toward a common goal, pressure situations, competition, respect for authority, creativity, critical thinking, problem-solving, communication, self-discipline, dependability, accountability, and focus. And a young athlete can experience all of the above in the first two games of a season! The challenge lies in helping our kids recognize these qualities and take ownership of those abilities to empower them toward living in greatness. I believe Warrior Parents can and will rise to that challenge, for we understand what's at stake is less about "me" and more about the mission: our children!

In the game of life, however, the rules, sportsmanship, and the definition of "winning" aren't that clear. And while youth sports strive for fairness, life is not always fair. Still, our kids are expected to survive and (hopefully) thrive, with the help of parents and other role models. At least that's how it's supposed to work.

This brings us to our challenge or "the mission, should you choose to accept it": Will you optimize sports' value and intentionally help your child develop as a person? This mission will require you to make adjustments, and, perhaps, a paradigm shift in the way you and your child approach sports. You and your child will have fun, learn, love, and grow together on the journey. Yes, I said *love*. You will love to watch your kid play, and he or she will experience your love via the quality time you spend together. And via the care, excitement, words of affirmation, and commitment you provide, regardless of the statistics or the won/loss record.

Remember, the core of parenting is love for your child. Love is why you are reading this book. You want the *Warrior Parent Playbook,* WP3 Sports Program, and WP3 Live in Greatness Application to provide your child the best possible life, both now and into the future.

2

PERSON OVER ATHLETE

"This is my dearly loved Son, who brings me great joy."

—MATTHEW 3:17 (NLT)

IN THE 2019 semifinals of the NCAA Women's College World Series, UCLA's Rachel Garcia threw 176 pitches and rang up 16 strikeouts in a 10-inning battle against Washington. She also hit a walk-off, three-run homer that launched her team into the CWS finals, against top-ranked Oklahoma. The Bruins swept the Sooners 2-0, with Garcia pitching both games. In the deciding contest, she struck out four and scattered eight hits, leading her team to a 5-4 win.

Garcia won the 2019 Honda Cup (given to the nation's top collegiate female athlete), and, for the second time, was named USA Softball Collegiate Player of the Year. She was also named National Fastpitch Coaches Association pitcher of the year,

ESPNW National Player of the Year, and Most Outstanding Player at the College World Series.[1]

Los Angeles Lakers star LeBron James (a 16-time All-Star) is the face of today's NBA. Since turning pro after high school, he has earned almost every accolade possible, from MVPs to World Championships to record-setting hundred-million-dollar contracts. His net worth is close to a half a billion dollars according to multiple sources. (His fortune includes many off-the-court ventures, such as the fast-growing Blaze Pizza chain and a stake in the Liverpool Football Club.)[2]

> Sports provide a platform where an athlete can feel loved by teammates and fans, where everyone's contributions matter. When you wear that jersey, you feel valued. You are encouraged to show what you're made of, and what you are capable of achieving.

And, of course, LeBron is in the thick of that GOAT (Greatest Of All Time) debate, with fellow NBA legends Michael Jordan, Magic Johnson, and Kobe Bryant.

Athletes like Rachel Garcia, LeBron, Tom Brady, and Alex Morgan are making the world realize sports' importance in the global culture. Athletes are celebrated and beloved by the masses. The world experienced a void during the stoppage of sports due to the global COVID-19 pandemic.

We have seen how many athletes' significance transcends what they do in competition. They are followed by millions on social media. People buy their jerseys, get tattoos, and even name their children Shaq, Kobe, or Lionel. This celebration of athletes cascades to college, high school, and youth sports, where the celebration and admiration is infectious, not only among the young athletes themselves, but also among coaches, parents, friends, and other family members who want the kids in their lives to have a positive experience.

Some parents commit thousands of hours (and thousands of dollars) so that their young athletes can enjoy the physical, mental, and social value of sports. Plus, sports are fun. Today's young athlete can enjoy an experience that mirrors (at least a little bit) that of his or her big-time sports heroes.

I know this, because I am a product of playing youth soccer, starting at age four in Cerritos, CA, back in the day. I also played myriad other sports, including two-hand touch football and "over-the-line" baseball in the streets, until the street lights came on, signaling the end of the game. I continued my athletic career for 17 more years, culminating with my days as a member of the UCLA Bruins football squad.

The "sports cycle" began again when I became a parent. I coached my kids in youth sports, starting with soccer when they turned four. It was a personal challenge for me to avoid following the culture that idolizes sport, allowing it to consume our lives by valuing performance and winning over personal development and fun. This competitive culture has devalued multi-sport participation and led to a growing movement of specializing in a sport at a young age, despite data that highlight the real risk of burnout and overuse injuries. Hence, young athletes and their parents can be seduced by the chase for a coveted athletic scholarship or by the status that accompanies a kid who is an "elite" athlete on a travel ball, club, or an AAU sports team. I believe (and I'm a living witness) that you can achieve both your athletic goals and personally develop children while having fun in multiple sports.

I had to learn from my own painful experiences of feeling devalued when I stepped outside the world of sports, with its euphoric and immediate gratification—as long as I was succeeding athletically. There were many times I didn't realize that I was loved for simply who I was. That I mattered, whether or not I excelled on the court or on the field.

So, as an adult, I committed with my wife to celebrate, invest in, and affirm our children: win or lose, in the uniform or out of it. This was an intentional effort to develop our kids holistically and strive for PERSONal development as we kept sports in their proper perspective.

I recall telling my sons, "You don't have to play football if you aren't having fun, but you will do some kind of extracurricular activity and work your butts off to be great at it." I firmly believe that greatness begins with the mindset that everyone can express the best version of him- or herself, regardless of the outcome. Regardless of how one athlete stacks up against the others. Children need to hear this truth over and over again, until they believe it and it becomes their standard. The time-tested principle of sowing and reaping applies here. Parents, what are we sowing into our children daily?

At their best, athletics provide a platform where an athlete can feel loved by teammates and fans, where everyone's contributions matter. When you wear that jersey, you feel valued. You are encouraged to show what you're made of, and what you are capable of achieving. These elements speak to the insatiable core desires of every human being:

» To know who you are

» To know you are valuable, that you matter

» To know what you are capable of

» To be part of a community—to form lasting relationships

Our young people want these things. More importantly, they need them. (Yes, things like marching band, cheerleading, dance, youth groups, and friendships can fill these needs too.) However, I am 100-percent convinced that sports are a uniquely great way to address these needs—and develop key life skills at the same time. These skills can be transferred over time from the athlete account to what I call the PERSONal account.

That's why I'm on a quest to coach, equip, and inspire parents to use sports to execute that transfer of life skills into their kids' personal development accounts. This will empower each child to live in greatness!

I believe that the best way to develop young athletes is to help them achieve the following:

» Athletic development: mobility, flexibility, strength, speed, footwork, agility, and conditioning

» Skill development: position drills, muscle memory, personal training, and extra backyard work

» Body development: nutrition, hydration, recovery, stretching, foam rolling, massage, etc.

» Mental development: Watch games "live" with a parent, coach, or teammates. Analyze film of games or practices, visualize high performance, and set goals.

All of this development complements the growth realized in the "routine" practices and games. It's "rinse and repeat," throughout the season, into the post- and preseason.

But what about a modus operandi (MO) to develop your child beyond the world of sports? In other words, what about the *other* 80 to 90 percent of their existence? If you have an MO, does it include understanding a child's strengths and weaknesses, personality profile, character development, listening to their heart's desires, and providing clear training about morality and ethics?

For example, how do we teach our kids to treat others? How do we help them grow spiritually, and understand their personal "love language?" How do we discern what makes our kids happy or sad? What do they fear? How do we expose them to the world in a responsible way?

The current global pandemic has forced parents and families to spend quality time together and reassess what's meaningful—without extracurricular activities.

But eventually, the games will resume. (Perhaps they already have for you and your family.) I believe sports can be a catalyst and a tool to personally develop your daughters and sons. This *Warrior Parent Playbook* and the WP3 Sports program (check out the section in the back of this book) can become a pivotal and intentional instrument that forges their personal development and empowers them to live in greatness.

Warriors in times past had to purposefully design and craft their arrows, for battle and/or hunting. When a warrior made an arrow, the intent was clear: To launch the arrow at a target with laser-like focus from a distance. I believe children are like arrows in the hands of parents. We want to craft and launch them so that they can soar toward their purpose. Throughout this book, I will use the arrow metaphor to illustrate the sports-based skills that you can integrate into your child's life. Each of the key life skills relates to the parts of an arrow:

> I firmly believe that greatness begins with the mindset that everyone can express the best version of him- or herself, regardless of the outcome. Regardless of how one athlete stacks up against the others.

Shaft (or Long Spine): Character

Arrowhead: Work Ethic/Hard Work, Self-Confidence, Growth Mindset/Personal Growth

Fletchings (or Feathers): Focus, Self-Discipline, Leadership, Competitive Drive, Grit, Passion, Healthy Lifestyle, Faith

Nock: Teamwork

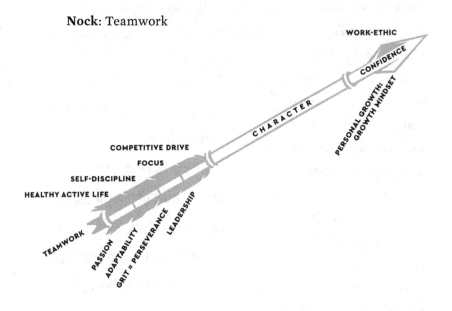

If you have a kid in sports, I hope you will continue to support him or her. However, I encourage you to make a paradigm shift that will optimize the sports experience *and* bring about new levels of personal development. Let's make this the "new normal" in youth and high school sports. Let's invest in our kids and celebrate them on the court or field and beyond. Let's help our kids feel confident and valued whether or not the uniform is on.

3

LIVING IN GREATNESS

*"Success is when I add value to myself.
Significance is when I add value to others."*

—JOHN MAXWELL[1]

"I AM THE GREATEST! I predict that [Sonny Liston] will go at eight to prove that I am great. If he wanna go to heaven, I'll get him in seven." If you are a longtime boxing fan, you may recall this 1964 quote from legendary boxer Muhammad Ali (Ali was known as Cassius Clay when he upset Liston to become the world heavyweight champion. He changed his name shortly after the fight.)[2]

The confident and boisterous Ali was absolutely right when he declared he was the greatest fighter of his era. We can argue whether he is the greatest boxer of *all time* (GOAT), but it's indisputable that Ali was cut from a unique cloth. We won't see another fighter like him. As the saying goes, "He was often imitated, never duplicated." [3]

With apologies to Mr. Ali, I must declare, however, that we are all unique. We are all cut from a personalized cloth, which includes all the materials we need to be great. Each living person is an example of one-of-a-kind workmanship. Think about it: Your DNA and your fingerprints are assigned only to you. No one can duplicate the original expression of you.

People like Muhammad Ali provide us a blueprint for living in our own unique greatness. If you live in greatness, you walk in the fullest and highest expression of *you*. In each moment, you strive to be the most authentic and best version of yourself. That's your gift to the world. It's a combination of your spirit, character, personality, gifts, life skills, and your own personal "secret sauce." Let that truth sink in. Living in greatness is not a destination; it's an ongoing growth journey that is expressed *daily*.

> If you live in greatness, you walk in the fullest and highest expression of you. In each moment, you strive to be the most authentic and best version of yourself. That's your gift to the world.

There are several keys to helping your child live in greatness. First, children must know they are loved and valued for who they are. (They need this affirmed daily; that's the WP3 recommended dosage). Your love should not be conditional. It should not be based on conformity. This conformity can create a caged bird with an unspoken song. As Maya Angelou proclaimed, "There is no greater agony than bearing an untold story inside you." [4]

Second, instill self-confidence in your children, and provide them the freedom to be authentic. They should know they are loved inside and out and be encouraged to share themselves with the world. I love how Beyonce inspired her daughters and (black girls globally) to do this in her *The Lion King: The Gift* soundtrack album. The song "Brown Skin Girl" affirms, "Brown skin girl / Your skin just like pearls / The best thing in the world / Never trade you for anybody else." [5]

Third, remember that sports are a great transformational platform to develop personal life qualities and skills that enhance a kid's greatness. The key is to intentionally help your child transfer those qualities from sports to the rest of life. If kids can show discipline on the field, the court, the mat, or the track, they can demonstrate discipline at home. They can make their bed every morning. They can clean up after themselves. Like a good coach, parents should set clear standards and expect that those standards will be met.

Don't let your kid get put into a "restricted athlete box," with all of its labels and stigmas. (Some people assume that athletes are spoiled, entitled, or one-dimensional.) We need to remind each kid, "You are more than an athlete." The best qualities exemplified in sports (such as work ethic, confidence, leadership, character, focus, adaptability, grit, and teamwork) should be invested into their personal life account, to be spent in all the places they are accepted—school, home, the neighborhood, youth group, workplace, parties, and so on. And, parents, we need to show our kids *how* to make those transfers.

Fourth, help your child live in greatness by teaching him or her to live in the *now*. It's impossible for a kid to passionately and purposefully express the best version of him- or herself without being fully present and engaged in each moment. This principle is best taught by parents who model it. I've struggled with this one myself (after all, I'm growing too), but I hope you can give your daughter or son a head start. What's more, living in the now will help build your relationship with your child because they will experience your full attention in each moment. (Of course, you can't always give a kid your full attention. In these instances, politely communicate this reality and explain how this kind of honesty actually shows the other person respect. It's more respectful, for example, to schedule a time to talk when you can give your kid your full attention, rather than pretending to listen while your mind is distracted by other priorities.)

Living in greatness is a powerful principle to teach your child, regardless of age. The tactics to implement this principle will vary depending on age and maturity level—and the nature of your existing relationship with your son or daughter. But trust me: Integrating this idea into your lives is worth the effort. (In fact, I encourage you to embark on this journey with your kids, even if they are not in sports.)

Remember, a kid's coach will expect the best and highest expression of their gifts and abilities—at practices and during games. You should feel empowered to hold those same expectations.

And remember that you are not alone on this journey. The WP3 community includes other parents and children who are participating with you. We all encourage and support each other. Living in greatness is something we should pursue daily. High-tech engineer Jim Keller reminds us how and why living in the moment is so important: "Say what you want to say when you have the feeling and the chance. My deepest regrets are the things I did not do, the opportunities missed and the things unsaid."[6]

LIVE IN YOUR GREATNESS!

4

THE WARRIOR PARENT MENTALITY

"Navy SEALs say when you are under pressure you don't rise to the occasion; you sink to the level of your training. Train Well!"

—JON GORDON[1]

OUR WORLD TODAY includes all kinds of adversity (including the current COVID-19 global pandemic), and leaders and citizens in every country are feeling unprecedented pressure.

Kids face pressure too, through social media, bullying, peer pressure, drugs, sex, crime, racism, gangs, and so much more. These pressures create moments of truth that reveal the level of a kid's "home" training. Just as the Navy SEALs train soldiers to prepare for the most extreme conditions and situations, we parents can teach principles based on the "Warrior Parent Mentality."

Before I describe this mentality as it relates to sports, I will clearly identify what it is *not*. It's not the extreme parent (usually a dad) who tries to live vicariously through a child. Some parents behave like the Dallas Cowboys or Los Angeles Lakers or Los Angeles Dodgers are scouting their 10-year-olds. Others insist on telling the coach how to use their kid so that he or she can be the team's MVP. (You'll often find these parents standing right next to the coach on the sidelines, trying to "coach" the coach!)

Then there are the parents who insist that their 10-year-old needs to focus on only one sport for the next 8 years—to increase the chance of getting a college scholarship. They make this choice for their kids, despite all of the well-documented benefits of multisport participation, benefits that include reducing the risk of burnout and overuse injuries.

And let's not forget the helicopter parent (usually Mom), who micromanages every detail of their young child's life. Those "details" often include the coach.

Some parents use foul language and are ready to fight at a youth sports game, all for the honor and dignity of "their team."

Such parents grab the news headlines and social-media attention, but I believe that most of us have good intentions when it comes to our young athletes. We seek a better way to develop our kids. That's what this *Warrior Parent Playbook* is all about.

What is a Warrior Parent Mentality? Here are three examples that reveal the kind of intentional mindset that helps a soldier, athlete, or child to survive and thrive in their assigned purpose.

Case 1: The US Navy SEAL instructor is responsible for designing a training regimen that will develop men and women into some of our mostly highly skilled soldiers for extreme missions. The attrition rate is 75 percent, meaning three out of every four who enroll will not finish their training.[2] Some of the elements stress-tested to the max during SEAL training are mental toughness, grit, leadership, focus, competitive drive, work ethic, discipline, confidence, personal growth, teamwork, physical and mental fitness, passion, and character.

Case 2: Coaches are responsible for designing training programs that involve SEAL-like life skills, right along with the offensive and defensive schemes, game fundamentals, techniques, and strategies for their players.

Case 3: Parents, you are responsible for having a parental strategy designed to personally develop your child for the game or mission called *life*. And of the three types of leaders noted here, you have the most important assignment. Remember, an athlete competes for a certain number of seasons, and a soldier serves for a tour (or tours) of duty. But the way you develop your child will be demonstrated for his or her entire lifetime, from the cradle to the grave.

You have the unique opportunity to help your child know and believe that their value comes from who they are, not from what they do. You can help them understand that their worth is not predicated on touchdowns, home runs, goals, points, 40-yard dash times, or any other statistic. At the core of every Warrior Parent is love for their child. If our children know and believe that they are valuable and loved by us and by God (or whatever you call your higher power) simply because they are *here*, they will develop into their best selves. They will be the greatest expression of themselves, for all the world to see and appreciate.

How do we develop this mindset and apply it to sports (or any competitive activity) as we help our kids acquire key life skills and live in greatness? It begins with our being "coachable." Just like a young athlete, we need to be able to receive and apply new teaching or instruction. Each of us must learn a principle and integrate it into our own personality. And we must embody each principle without compromising its integrity. As my kids' Brazilian soccer coach, Dennis, would say about how to apply what you've learned in practice to live games, "You are not robots; football is 'O Jogo Bonito' (the beautiful game), and is played with personality and flare and life."

The Warrior Parent Mentality involves our accepting the responsibility to parent the *person,* as we allow the coach to assume his or her role and responsibility for the player and team. It's unfair to expect coaches to parent your child, while you play the role of "friend." Yes, some coaches coach "from the inside out," focusing on character and other life skills. But coaches like this should supplement and support your role, not usurp it.

Warrior Parents want their kids to be equally self-confident in or out of the uniform. We see how Captain America (aka Steve Rogers) didn't need his red, white, and blue suit to have super strength, speed, leadership abilities, or keen instincts; however, the suit did make him look super cool.

The WP3 sports program features several ways to help parents and their kids

> It's unfair to expect coaches to parent your child, while you play the role of "friend." Coaches should supplement and support your role, not usurp it.

achieve their goals. For example, I encourage you to alter the scorecard for your child. If you're familiar with sports, you know about the scorecard (or game grade), which measures team and individual stats like base hits, home runs, stolen bases, and strikeouts in baseball or softball—or touchdowns, rushing yards, tackles, sacks, and interceptions in football. These tools are a good way to measure performance on the field. However, there is a different (and more important) scorecard you should pursue. Every child can excel by this measure, which focuses on the person more than the athlete. This scorecard could measure the following:

» Work ethic, grit, competitive drive, focus, and teamwork (on the field, court, or mat)

and/or

» Confidence, gratitude, service, learning something new (at school)

If you create this type of scorecard (and post it on the refrigerator or bedroom wall), you will encourage growth in all of the areas you measure. (I recommend a rating of 1, 2, or 3, rather than letter grades. Also, rate things that you and your child agree are important. This rating system creates a great opportunity for intentional conversation and provides metrics for growth and accountability.

Every three weeks, alter the categories. (Dr. Maxwell Maltz notes, "It takes 21 days to develop a new habit.") [3] I understand this will require some parental adjusting, depending on your priorities and your child's age. However, once you get started, remain consistent. As the process gains momentum, you will begin to see a difference in your child.

PRESENCE, POWER, AND PURPOSE

A warrior's calling requires him or her to be fully present in the now, to leave no room for complacency when engaged in the mission. Warriors live authentically and give the best of themselves. They activate their inner power and channel it toward their purpose in a given moment. Why? The mission is at stake. Victory or defeat (and sometimes life or death) is at stake.

When an athlete is fully present, we sometimes call it putting on the "game face" or being "in the zone." Actors refer to it as getting "in character." Entertainers like Beyonce seem to transform from a mere mortal to a force of nature when they hit the stage.

Parents, let's embrace the Warrior Parent Mentality and activate it daily, so that we can be present for our kids.

Given all of life's activities and the many responsibilities on your plate, I know it's challenging to operate in presence, power, and purpose with your kids. Sometimes, all the stuff that is supposed to give us a rich and fulfilling life can distract us from the treasures found only in the now, in those moments where we and our families can experience love, joy, laughter, vitality, sadness, triumph, freedom, and peace by living fully and authentically. Sometimes we fail to notice the birds in the morning, living out their purpose by singing melodies to heaven, inspiring all who are able to hear and appreciate the beauty of the universe.

Sometimes we don't pause to recognize the color purple in a blossoming flower and smile gratefully.

Being present means watching your child's mood change from gloom to sunshine after a defeat when you say, "I loved watching you play today. It's inspiring how you never give up and always fight as hard as you can until the last whistle."

Yes, operating in full presence, power, and purpose is about you, but it's more about your impacting someone else's life by sharing the fullness of your gifts and your best self with them.

How do we get to this level and stay there? Our greatest barrier is often ourselves. Brendon Burchard states, "Our only enemy in this effort is ourselves. To gain greater presence, we will need to overcome our habit of living in the past or future.

And we will need to become more aware of the roles and responsibilities we can choose each and every moment as free, conscious, motivated people." [4]

To gain this awareness, we start by blocking out life's distractions and focusing on the target. If you watch an expert archer in action, you'll notice how they close one eye to narrow their focus on the target. So, what do *you* need to close an eye to in order to sharpen your focus?

I encourage you to ask your child how he or she focuses, whether she's a softball player in the batter's box, a point guard at the free-throw line, or a soccer midfielder taking a penalty kick. Every sport provides those moments when it's essential to operate in presence, power, and purpose. Good coaches know when a player is in the zone or suffering from a mental lapse. (You can't mentally check out on the field or take a "play off" with coaches like this.)

> Being present means watching your child's mood change from gloom to sunshine after a defeat when you say, "I loved watching you play today. It's inspiring how you never give up and always fight as hard as you can until the last whistle."

Similarly, as parents we can help our kids recognize when they are operating in presence, power, and purpose—and when they are not. We can let them know when they make a bad decision because their mind was somewhere else (perhaps in the past or the future instead of in the moment.)

When we operate in presence, power, and purpose, we live in greatness. I strive to live in greatness, and my wife/co-head coach appreciates that version of me, versus when I take moments off. I tell my kids every day, "Live in your greatness! Unleash it! Live in a state where the best and most authentic version of yourself is expressed unapologetically."

As a parent, model and uphold this standard in your family. It will take time and mental discipline to get there. But your children (and the increased quality of life) are worth the work. Remember, the *Warrior Parent Playbook* is designed to help all kids live in their greatness, develop skills to succeed in life, and strengthen the family unit. Let's do this one day and one moment at a time, together!

THE MARATHON MINDSET

A marathon, 26.2 miles, is a race of pain and pleasure. It's a bucket-list item for a few of us, but certainly not most of us. For marathoners, the race marks a transformative season in life, and it often shatters what someone thought he or she was capable of achieving. The "marathon mindset" is something Warrior Parents can learn and incorporate into their lives.

During the months of marathon training, runners (many of them non-athletes) push themselves beyond their known physical and mental limits. They grow and learn so much about themselves on the journey. This training is rarely done alone. It often requires a running group (or at least a partner or two) to stay encouraged and to crush each milestone *together*.

Like a running partner, we parents must see beyond our children's limits and encourage them to stay the course, so that they realize what they are capable of achieving.

For example, if your child decides to play a sport, there is no quitting during the season if things get tough. Why? The marathon mindset recognizes that life will bring challenges and difficult times. One can't take the easy way out and quit. Instead, encourage your kids to realize that adversity and obstacles are an opportunity to develop perseverance, endurance, and grit.

Here's a personal example of the marathon mindset. Since my younger son, Elisha, was 3 ½ years old, we have intentionally moved him up to compete at the next highest age level in his sports. This allowed him to compete with his older brother, and it forced him to persevere and work extra hard to earn playing time.

It all paid off by his freshman year of high school. Because of the work ethic, grit, confidence, competitive drive, and focus, Elisha transformed from a freshman-team starter to starting on the varsity team at Cedar Park High School. He was able to play with his older brother for the last eight games of the season, culminating with the Texas 5A State Championship game at the Dallas Cowboys AT&T Stadium in Arlington. (The team lost in the finals that year, but went 16-0 and won the state title the following year.). Fastforward to his junior year in high school: Although Elisha wasn't able to earn much playing time on the varsity basketball team, his motivating attitude, work ethic at practice, and leadership were recognized when he received a Player of the Month award. Remember, parents, it's more about who they become on the journey, not just the statistical score-card of playing time and recruiting "stars" ratings.

The marathon mindset allows you to enjoy the moment but always keep *the mission* in mind. In the book *Grace Over Grind*, author Shae Bynes notes that a marathon's mile markers and water stations are necessary (and refreshing), but they are not the objective. The objective is who runners will become during the marathon so that they can cross the finish line. Likewise, for a high school student, the key objective is not to pass a test or achieve perfect atten-dance. The real mission is to cross that graduation stage

> **Enjoy the moment, but always keep the mission in mind.**

with maturity and life skills, as the best version of him- or herself, prepared for a life of significance and success.

I like how UCLA's legendary Coach John Wooden explains it: "Be concerned with your preparation, not theirs; your execu-tion, not theirs; your effort and desire, not theirs. Don't worry about them. Let them worry about you."[5]

In other words, people should look out for the child you are sending off into the world, not the other way around.

5

RAISING SUPERHEROES

HE SACRIFICED and fought for a cause bigger than himself.

He used his gifts and abilities for the benefit of others.

He courageously acted in the face of opposition.

He overcame the fear of failure.

He inspired others to hope in the best of humanity.

It might sound like I am describing a big-screen superhero like Captain America or Batman or Black Panther, but I'm actually describing my dad—my coach, my teacher, and my hero.

My dad exhibited all those traits, and more. He stood above all those superheroes I saw at the movies. He wasn't perfect, but he was *real*. He believed in me and told me I could do anything in life. Yep, that's right. My dad, the son of a Louisiana sharecropper, became a superhero. He lived a life filled with significance. I, my brother, and so many others are evidence that he was here and he crushed the mission assigned to him.

Raising young superheroes doesn't involve magical events or super serums. It's about intentional choices, empowering words, and a commitment to use sports as a training ground.

Let's start with those intentional choices. In Marvel's superhero action films, there is always a villain. The villain is usually greedy and selfish, concerned only with benefiting himself. In contrast, the superhero represents a selfless cause of great significance, something that benefits others and restores balance in the world, for the good of all humanity.

Let's translate this contrast to sports: We need to encourage young athletes to intentionally choose to put the team's goals above their own, without compromising their gifts in any way. Encourage your kid, "Play hard and do your best for your teammates, not for your own glory." Let's train our children to choose creative and selfless ways to be significant, and to exceed expectations and responsibilities. For example, after an "away game," maybe your son can help the home team clean up the field. Or, encourage your daughter to be a "servant leader" by getting to the field early before practices and games to help with the set-up. Maybe you and your child can organize opportunities for players who want to put in extra work and improve their games. Be creative. How can you show your child how to choose to bring significance to others' lives?

Now let's talk about empowering words, a key to building young superheroes. A parent's words are so crucial to a young person's development at any stage. There is a proverb that speaks to this very point: "The tongue has the power of life and death, and those who love it will eat its fruit" (Proverbs 18:21 NIV). What we say as parents can cultivate and activate life in our children, or be a discouragement that wounds their self-confidence. I learned this the hard way early on, when I coached my kids' teams in soccer, football, basketball, and track.

As a coach, my post-game critical approach discouraged my kids, and my wife had to firmly remind me that they needed a *dad* after the games. They needed me to speak words of love, encouragement, celebration, and life into them. I could assume the coach role and work on improvements later on, at practice.

The lesson is twofold:

1. Words have power to build up or tear down your child.

2. Children need parents who speak love, affirmation, celebration into their lives, parents who believe in each child's individual greatness. If you consistently take this approach, you will produce your very own superhero.

We can use sports as the primary training platform for raising superheroes, because athletics provide a plethora of life lessons. Through sports, kids learn teamwork and how to strive toward a common vision. They learn to overcome adversity through grit, and to conquer unforeseen challenges through adaptability. They learn to make a healthy lifestyle a priority, as being healthy allows you to give your best to others, in your sport and beyond.

And here are two more vital life lessons from sports, lessons that will empower your child with lifelong superpowers:

1. **Sports dismantle the fear of failure**. They provide a perfect platform for helping kids realize they don't need to fear failure, because sports are about trial and error. Do you know Michael Jordan's career three-point shooting percentage? It is 32.7 percent. That's right; the great Michael Jordan made less than one-third of his three-pointers.[1] So why shouldn't a young athlete take the shot or swing the bat? Why not take the action in life?

A young baseball or softball player learns to swing the bat and not be afraid.

Here's why: Even in major league baseball, you can strike out or otherwise fail to get a base hit most of the time and still be an all-star. (In 2019, Chicago White Sox shortstop Tim Anderson led all of major league baseball with a .335 batting average.) Yes, for us non-math majors, that means you need to get a hit only 3 out of 10 times to be considered a really good batter.[2] This is because hitting a baseball is one of sports' greatest challenges. The pitches come at different speeds, and there are many different types of pitches (curveball, slider, knuckleball, fastball, and more). Some pitchers are right-handed; others are lefties. So, your child goes to the plate and tries over and over again, facing adversity and the fear of failure. That takes superhero determination and confidence.

In pro basketball, a player can miss about half of his shots and be a league leader in field goal percentage, especially if we are talking about three-pointers. (Just watch the "Splash Brothers": Stephen Curry and Klay Thompson of the Golden State Warriors play.) [3]

Here's my point, parents: Your child, in whatever sport he or she plays, learns to laugh in the face of failure dozens of times every week, and they are taught to learn and grow from it. What if they adopt this attitude in the rest of life? In relationships, public speaking, applying for a scholarship, or starting an online business? Whatever the endeavor, sports help kids avoid the fear of failure. Instead, they practice, they learn, they believe, and they find a way to make it happen. Even if they "strike out" 7 out of ten times. Sports help us teach our kids, to quote former Los Angeles mayor Tom Bradley, "The only thing that will stop you from fulfilling your dreams is you." [4]

Let's help our kids believe that when they strike out, they will get a hit the next time up.

2. Sports encourage and enable personal growth.

One of sports' pillars is the quest to always be improving your game, always striving to master your craft. This is another way that athletes resemble those movie superheroes; they are always looking for ways to improve. Iron Man and Black Panther get new suits, while Wonder Woman trains among the Amazons of Themyscira.

These characters understand that the challenges and (sometimes) the opponent will be different every time. What worked last year probably won't work this time around.

Sports are like that. You face a different team (or different opponent) each week. (And even if you face the same team twice or more in a season, it will likely be a better version of that team.) That's why the focus on improvement and personal growth is paramount. In sports, growth comes through regular practices and through extra work and mental exercises with a personal trainer, batting coach, parent, older sibling, etc.

Sports' growth mindset applies to all of life's other domains: relationships, academics, social settings, faith, and so much more.

Children need parents who speak love, affirmation, celebration into their lives, parents who believe in each child's individual greatness. If you consistently take this approach, you will produce your very own superhero.

This mindset should be natural for your child to adopt. After all, growth begins with things like a toddler figuring out that the square peg does not fit into the round hole (or how to use a stool to reach the cookie jar on the counter).

Parents, let's apply the growth mindset (cultivated through sports) to our kids' personal lives and watch them live in greatness and become a real-life superhero to someone.

What if raising young people to become superheroes and live lives of significance became the norm within youth and high school sports? Why can't it be? Why can't it start with your child's team pursuing this goal through WP3? What barriers do we need to overcome to make total-person development the norm in all youth sports? Isn't that the nature and mission of being a superhero: to break free from the norm and create a better life for the next generation? My fellow Warrior Parents, the alarms are louder than ever in the world that awaits your children, and I believe raising superheroes through sports is the best way to answer the call. And you are not alone; there are others who will join you on this quest to raise superheros. There are resources to make this a reality. The Chinese philosopher Laozi said, "A journey of a thousand miles started with a first step." [5] Let's take each step together!

6

THE POWER OF DREAMING

"There is only one thing that makes a dream impossible to achieve: the fear of failure."

—PAULO COELHO, *The Alchemist*[1]

THE POWER of dreaming has been evident since the beginning of time, and we can still see that power today, enacted through so many lives.

In ancient Sparta, warriors were trained, equipped, and mentally conditioned to imagine that their greatest glory was in battle against a worthy opponent, for a cause greater than themselves.

Joseph, a son of Jacob, dreamed he would rule over an entire kingdom and help millions of people through periods of famine.

A little boy from Baltimore, Maryland, named Michael Phelps, dared to dream he could swim in the Olympics, stand on the podium with an American flag over his shoulder, and win gold medals. He finished his career with 23 gold medals (28 total medals), making him the most decorated summer Olympian of all time! [2]

Alex Morgan, a young girl from sunny Southern California, dreamed of shining in her sport (soccer) and winning a World Cup for Team USA, hoisting that historic trophy above her head. She has led the American team to two World Cup titles, and her career is not over yet.

The possibilities for your child are limitless, whether they're from Greece, Israel, Maryland, or California. Greatness like Phelps's or Morgan's began with a dream, a vision of accomplishing something bigger than oneself. And these athletes have made a huge impact on so many people, even those beyond sports. I love how Oprah Winfrey puts it: "The most important journey of our lives doesn't necessarily involve climbing the highest peak or trekking around the world. The biggest adventure you can ever take is to live the life of your dreams." [3]

Warrior Parents, I'm calling on you to help your child to live the life of their dreams. Each and every one of our children have a dream, a significant purpose buried inside of them. Let's pause and reflect on this truth for a minute before we move on.

As I write this, our two sons are living out their childhood dreams of playing football at UCLA and playing in the NFL, while our daughter decided late in high school that she wanted to be a pediatrician and is now a pre-med honor-roll student at San Diego State University. There is no greater joy as a parent than to see your children's journey as they live out and enjoy the experience of their dreams, big or small.

I need you to believe this truth about your child's purpose, despite your current situation or circumstances in life. It is imperative that we parents listen to our kids' hearts and encourage them to dream with no boundaries. Let's give them permission to fail on their journey. As we have already learned, failure is part of growth and learning.

In your kids' dreams, you will see their gifts and passions. You will realize how life's adversities mold them into the person who can achieve the dream. No one should block, discourage, or deter a child from his or her dreams, especially not Mom or Dad.

I must emphasize that we are talking about a child's dreams, not ours. Too many times I have seen kids pursuing Mom's or Dad's dreams, not their own. Some parents try to achieve their unfulfilled dreams through a son or daughter, trying to live vicariously through their children. Parents, we must realize that each child is one-of-a-kind, uniquely made with dreams and a purpose in life. Our role is to help our kids unlock and live in their greatness and be true to their hearts. We should support them so they can passionately pursue their dreams.

Encourage your child to spend time dreaming, imagining, and envisioning—with no smartphones or other distractions around. You can feed a kid's dream by exposing him or her to what's possible. Help them explore and understand the various career paths available to them. This can be achieved through movies or documentaries, field trips, online research, job-shadowing, internships, volunteer opportunities, etc.

As you help your child dream and explore possibilities, be prepared to engage with them and understand what's resonating with them. Help them turn that dream into a vision and then a plan.

For example, in an elementary school assignment, Steve Harvey wrote that he wanted to be rich and appear on TV when he grew up. At the time, he didn't know how he was going to get there. But a seed had been planted, and, despite lots of opposition and obstacles, he found his gifting: comedy. He worked extremely hard and eventually blossomed into living his dream of being a successful comedian and TV star.

So, don't stifle the seeds. Cultivate them. On a child's journey toward their best self, their focus will narrow, and they will develop the life skills to help them live their dreams.

Don't allow society to label or limit your child's possibilities, and please don't expect schools to unlock a child's dreams. Yes, that *can* happen, with an extraordinary teacher, counselor, or coach, but that's not a school's primary responsibility.

I believe you have the Warrior Parent Mentality to stir up, nurture, and cultivate the best of what's inside your child. You create the conditions for success in your child's life. It's the power of your love and the power of your words of life that will enable them to thrive, to launch, and soar toward their dreams. Believe me when I say there is no greater joy than seeing your child work hard, grow, and fulfill their goals and dreams in life.

In competitive sports, we hear a lot about having a vision or visualizing oneself achieving something great. When one season ends, the coach often creates a vision for the next season. The coach hopes that the team will embrace that vision.

A vision usually is a "stretch goal," something that will force each athlete to grow and be at their best. This creates an environment of striving toward excellence, intense competition, and consistent growth.

In 2016, Leicester City accomplished the biggest shock in English Premier League football history by winning their league title, against 5000-1 odds (one loyal and now handsomely paid fan made that bet before the season), and while offering the lowest team salary in the league. It all started with a belief in a vision. According to Claudio Ranieri, the team's manager, "I am very happy to win, because when you start to make a manager you hope you can win some league. I won the most important league in Europe, [and] I think, not just Europe, but the world, the Premier League. It is a fantastic achievement. . . ." [4]

So, let's raise our kids' trajectory! It is important to encourage a high trajectory toward any goal. After all, no one but God truly knows their potential. I realized long ago that mediocrity and excellence *both* require making a choice (and then a series of choices daily). Have you heard this saying? "If you shoot for

> **"The key is not to worry about being successful but to instead work toward being significant—and the success will naturally follow."**
>
> **—WINTLEY PHIPPS**

the tree in front of you, you'll hit it every time, but if you shoot for the moon you might hit a star, even if you miss." In both cases, you need to take your shot.

Remember, your goal is to help kids live in greatness, and dreaming plays an integral part on that journey to excellence. I encourage you to dream too—and share with your kids precisely how you are pursuing (and living) your dreams. I wrote this book and created a sports program that originates from a dream and vision of positively impacting children, parents, and families across the world through my core passions of faith, family, sports, and coaching. I have shared (maybe too much at times) this journey with "my kids" with the hope they will pursue their dreams and passions in life, no matter how old they are.

If you are here on planet Earth, you have a purpose. The best way to encourage dreaming in your child is to model it. Give kids access to your life story. You never know how your story will inspire a kid to achieve greatness and remove limitations like the fear of failure or worrying about what others might think. For example, my wife, Dr. MamaKai, unlocked a dream later in life, and, after spending 14 years as a stay-at-home mom (a great one, I must add), she went to medical school and became a physician. Her journey, courage, and resilience inspired me and our kids to DREAM BIG! Singer Wintley Phipps puts it best: "The key is not to worry about being successful but to instead work toward being significant—and the success will naturally follow." [5]

7

CRAFTING ARROWS THAT SOAR

"Children born to a young man are like arrows
in a warrior's hands."

—SOLOMON (PSALM 127:4 NLT)

FROM LEGOLAS, the Sindarin Elf in *Lord of the Rings*, to Katniss Everdeen in *The Hunger Games*, to Hawkeye in *The Avengers*, to the Amazon women in *Wonder Woman*, these fictional characters are brave warriors who possess amazing archery skills. Given all of that courage and skill, I wonder who made the arrows, and for what purpose: battle or hunting. An arrow's long shaft must have the right length and be made of the right materials if it is to soar effectively. And an arrowhead must be sharp and strong enough to pierce its intended target (armor, walls, or flesh and bone). Some arrowheads include explosives or poison, depending on their use.

Then there are the fletchings (or feathers) on the tail end of the shaft. They are designed to steer and aerodynamically stabilize the arrow once it's launched. The fletchings keep the arrow in proper alignment as it cuts through the resistance of natural elements like wind, rain, and gravity.

Lastly, the nock is attached to the bottom tip of the shaft, below the fletchings. According to George Tekmitchov, a senior engineer at Easton Archery, "Arrow nocks are pretty amazing. These small, plastic parts are expected to take the full force of each shot and transmit that force to the arrow shaft in exactly the same way, over and over again."

> **Love enables us to enjoy the process, every day. Love relishes progress, even slow progress.**

The mindful and purposeful design of the arrow is paramount to the cause the warriors are engaged in; a cause bigger than themselves. A warrior understands that each arrow will impact the cause, one shot at a time.

I love the way Dr. MamaKai (my wife and the mother of our three children) puts it: "A warrior has the skill, the mindset, and the wisdom to know exactly what to do with an arrow."

Parents, you are that warrior. Your children are the arrows, and this *Warrior Parent Playbook* is a way to use sports to shape, forge, weld, and personally develop your child to live in individual greatness. Of course, parenting a free-willed young person is not an exact science. However, we can learn some core principles by exploring how arrows were made before technology and advanced machinery.

First, design and build with love. Love enables us to enjoy the process, every day. Love relishes progress, even slow progress.

Second, remember that discipline is key in developing an arrow. Discipline is the consistent and firm faithfulness to a standard that shapes each specific part of the arrow. For example, the arrowhead will require another hard substance to shape and sharpen it, while the fletchings require a more gentle (yet equally precise) approach.

So we must choose our methods wisely and be clear and consistent about our standards for our kids. We must follow a developmental mindset, one that engages, understands, processes, and applies the best method and tool for each moment, depending on which part of the "arrow" we are crafting. Speak life and purpose into your arrows daily. Remind them how they matter. Remind them what they are capable of.

Below is a detailed picture of the WPP arrow and how it correlates to specific life skills that are developed through sports. (Please note that these are not the only qualities developed in sports, but ones I've seen help people realize their fullest potential.)

Shaft or long spine: the core of the arrow

CHARACTER

Arrowhead: the sharp, indestructible, piercing part of the arrow

Fletching: the aerodynamic stabilizing and alignment part of the arrow

Nock: the connecting part between the warrior and arrow, which transmits the force to propel the arrow FORWARD

Bonus Instinct: the sustaining belief that launching your arrow will make an impact

Raising children who will significantly impact the world is not for the faint of heart. It requires a Warrior Parent Mentality and a playbook to help keep things on track. The intentional holistic development of the total person in sports includes all participants, regardless of athletic talent or individual success. The target is clear for each child: Live in your own personal greatness. Live toward your purpose. That's what will impact others.

Parents, enjoy the journey of seeing these life skills play out each week as you watch your daughter or son play sports (or any competitive activity). Embrace the task of developing these skills in them, because these skills can improve all domains of a young person's life.

SECTION
TWO

DEVELOPING LIFE SKILLS

8

THE SHAFT/LONG SPINE: CHARACTER

CHADWICK BOSEMAN in *Black Panther*; Emma Stone in *La La Land*; Viola Davis in *Fences*; Joaquin Phoenix in *Joker*; Denzel Washington in *Training Day*. Actors who give signature performances like these must choose a script that speaks to them. Then they read and understand the story, embody the essence of the role, and "live" a character we will never forget.

Some performers identify so strongly with their characters that they find it hard to put the role aside and live a normal life once a day's shooting is complete. For example, after playing the villain Erik Killmonger in *The Black Panther*, actor Michael B. Jordan sought therapy to "unpack" the lonely place he took himself into in order to embody that unsavory character's nature.

Parents, let's be conscious that we are the directors in our kids' "movie." We are responsible for writing the script and helping to shape our children's character. But how do we do this without polluting or stifling the distinct nature that make sons and daughters who they are? There is no single right answer. However, we can see the *wrong* answers—answers that are expressed through hate, racism, sexism, bullying, etc. Underneath these attitudes lie insecurity, fear, and pride.

Sports show us that you can win convincingly or lose a close match and still do it with sportsmanship, the character-driven component in sports. Sports show how we can value our teammates and our opponents. We can adopt this principle in life as we seek to value and understand those with different skin colors, religions, or socioeconomic backgrounds. This is one of the true treasures of sports.

Sports embody many character-enriching components: self-control, respect, honor, fairness, love, responsibility, dependability, and more. But these qualities can be easier to express on the court, pitch, mat, or field. Roles are very clear. Teammates, opponents, coaches, and officials are clearly identified.

But what happens when there is no scoreboard, time clock, or supervisors present? The stuff that happens in the 90 percent of life that occurs beyond athletics. What happens when a young athlete's character is tested and there is no coach, teammate, referee, or league official around? How can we be confident that our kids will display the kind of character that will make us proud, and, more importantly, enhance the world? There are answers in the universe that we can draw from.

Character is the aggregate of features and traits that form the individual nature of someone or something. The distinct nature of a Sequoia tree in California's Yosemite National Park provides guidance on how to personally develop character in our children. At the height of a 26-story building (286 feet tall) and the width of a city street (30 feet wide), this living organism has massive "character" that allows it to withstand the storms and pressures of life while radiating beauty and glory and fresh oxygen (its purpose) for others to enjoy.

> "Gratitude blocks toxic emotions, such as envy, resentment, regret, and depression, which can destroy our happiness. It's impossible to feel envious and grateful at the same time."
>
> —DR. ROBERT EMMONS

To fully appreciate the divine character of a Sequoia tree, you must examine the part no one else can see, the part that gets dirty: the roots! The roots of a Sequoia tree go as deep as 12 feet and are matted together, covering a width up to an acre. (Pause for a moment to imagine an acre's worth of roots, deeper than most swimming pools, which support and feed the distinct character we see and experience in a tree.) With the right amount water, sunlight, space, and nutrients, this tree grows to embody its distinct greatness and glory.[1]

I think you see where I am going with this analogy: Parents, we do the work in our homes (underground), where the outside world can't see. We consistently nourish our kids' roots.

We provide healthful nutrients (love, kindness, self-control, respect, joy, etc.). We pour water (life lessons) daily into and over their character, and we provide the space to expand to each child's potential.

This involves getting into the trenches and influencing what shapes a kid's character, including what they watch, listen to, and ingest online, as well as the people they spend time with. As noted in Scripture, "Bad company corrupts good character." (1 Corinthians 15:33 NIV). My wife and I have created a Guidry Code of Conduct, and you can do the same thing in your household. As you set your standards, be mindful that the goal is to develop the person (their heart and their roots), not just behavior. This is accomplished by focusing less on the behavior or "symptom," and more on the "why." Seek to understand and influence what is going on with the person *inside. That will enable you to address and treat the"roots"to break cycles of self-destructive decisions and behaviors.*

As parents, there are many important character traits and values that we need to teach our children: honesty, friendliness, compassion, trustworthiness, faithfulness, work ethic, empathy, and so on. As James Kerr reminds us, "Our values determine our character. Our character decides our worth."[2] So where do we begin? The four "value pillars" (love, humility, integrity, and gratitude) are a great place to start. Let's explore each of these foundational values.

Love is a powerful value. Love is a choice, as well as an emotion. Humans innately long for love: to receive it and to give it. We seek to fill our insatiable need for love through friends, sports, academics, business, money, and fame, as well as through accumulating followers and "likes" on social media. However, when it comes to our kids, parents are the most important source of L.O.V.E. As a parent, you have the power to fill your child with so much love, especially the unconditional kind that feeds their roots and the core of their being with the sustenance that comes from knowing, "I am valuable. I matter."

It is important to note three guidelines here:

1. A kid's value should not be based on circumstances, because no one can control all circumstances. But you can choose to love and value your kids unconditionally, which includes discipline as an expression of love.

2. Don't create a performance-based love relationship. This might cause your child to fear failure and limit their ambitions. They might learn to believe that they can never meet your standards, which means they can never earn (or keep) your love.

3. Model the essence of love for others by teaching your kids to "treat people the way you want to be treated."

Warrior Parents, I must stress the vital role love plays in creating a person of character, beyond sports. Love will help your child develop Sequoia-like strength and lasting character.

And let's teach our kids humility (pillar 2), which is a great catalyst for personal growth. Humility means being coachable and having a servant's heart. I like how Rick Warren describes it: "Humility is not thinking less of yourself, it's thinking of yourself less."[3]

Humility softens the hardness of pride and removes the blinders of ego—barriers that stifle personal growth and prevent us from learning from others.

Yes, we want our young athletes to be confident, in and out of the uniform—and regardless of whether they are a five-star college prospect or a "role player." But we can help them be simultaneously confident *and* humble by encouraging them to do the "little things" for others. For example, New Zealand's legendary All Blacks rugby team reinforces humility by having teammates take turns "sweeping the sheds" (cleaning the locker room). This communicates to every player, "Never be too big to do the small things that must be done."

A humble player asks the coach, "How can I do better as a leader, a teammate?" As parents, we need to help our soccer, softball, football, basketball, baseball, rugby, etc. players answer this question: "How can I be better as a person?"

This brings us to pillar 3: gratitude, a transformative value that has mental, emotional, and spiritual impact. Being thankful sharpens our focus and broadens our perspective. A grateful person appreciates what he has, rather than obsessively comparing himself to others and what they have. (This is very important in youth sports, where a young athlete might encounter a teammate or opponent who is athletically gifted beyond belief and/or has parents who can afford personal trainers and coaches and access to world-class training facilities.)

Gratitude enables children to see the positive in situations. Instilling a sense of gratitude was a game changer for our children, but it took intentional work, with Dr. MamaKai doing most of the heavy lifting. Specifically, we taught our kids to be grateful for *each* opportunity to play, for their abilities, for their coaches, and for a mom who drove them all around town for practices, training, and games.

This focus on thankfulness slayed the "entitlement bandit" that robs many young athletes of their joy, and it showed our sons and daughter that they should never take people or opportunities for granted. Psychologist Robert Emmons (an expert on the science of gratitude) highlights additional benefits of gratitude: "Gratitude blocks toxic emotions, such as envy, resentment, regret, and depression, which can destroy our happiness. It's impossible to feel envious and grateful at the same time." He adds that gratitude allows a person to "celebrate the present . . . be more stress-resilient and strengthen social ties and self-worth." [4]

How can you encourage gratitude in your house? Buy or create a daily or weekly "gratitude journal." That's a good start. Or simply use dinner time to go around the table and ask each person to talk about something he or she is grateful for.

Our final pillar, integrity, is the quality of being honest and having strong moral principles. A person of integrity does the right things, even when no one is watching. This character pillar can be taught, but it's best to model it.

Integrity reveals itself even in the little details, such as failing to touch each line on the volleyball court when running "suicide" sprints. Or failing to put the toys away because Mom and Dad aren't home to supervise.

But people who cut corners with the small stuff tend to do the same thing on matters of great importance. UCLA basketball coach John Wooden was spot-on when he said, "Ability may get you to the top, but it takes character to keep you there."[5] Remember, we want to raise children who soar toward their purpose, but we also want them to have the character that will keep them flying high.

SUMMARY

1. Sports will contribute to character development through sportsmanship and "code of conduct" pledges, but we parents have the ultimate responsibility and power to shape our kids' character

2. Love, humility, gratitude, and integrity are strong character roots. They will help build massive, Sequoia-like character in your children.

3. Character is more important than winning, losing, 5-Star ratings, or any other statistical metrics. On your kids' "life scorecard," make character the most important metric!

4. Resist the temptation to be a "helicopter parent." Instead, teach and model good behavior and allow your child the space to grow into his or her potential.

ACTIONABLE DEVELOPMENT

» What small tasks can your child (and teammates) do that seem unimportant but are necessary for team success, or that simply help someone else at a time of need?

» Talk to your kids about their friends. Let them articulate what they like about these people. Do they have similar aspirations and values? If not, what advice and direction can you provide?

PERSONAL APPLICATION

Affirmation:

>> Look for opportunities to affirm and mirror kids' character traits back to them. This will help them understand who they are, what they are capable of, and that they *matter*.

>> Affirm traits such as love, humility, gratitude, and integrity throughout their everyday activities and interactions with others. In other words, "Catch your kids doing something right."

Acknowledge:

>> Identify and communicate when you see your child display strong character traits at home, or in their sport.

>> Highlight strong character traits when you watch a movie or athletic event together.

>> Show kids how their character is growing stronger. Be aware of the "teachable moments" that allow you to do this.

Reward:

>> Celebrate their high character, especially when it's demonstrated in the face of adversity. Commend them for helping others.

9

THE ARROWHEAD:
WORK ETHIC/HARD WORK!

Whatever you do, work at it with all your heart....

—COLOSSIANS 3:23 NIV

TO TRULY LIVE in greatness and soar in life, hard work is an absolute necessity. Among all of the life skills, I have special love for work ethic, because it requires no talent. Further, it is something that can be learned over time. It's a deep conviction that anyone can develop, through desire and perseverance.

I learned important lessons about work ethic when I was coaching a team of 11- to 13-year-old boys in tackle football. We had just finished an undefeated season and won the league championship. My team featured seven players who would go on to play Division 1 sports, including football, basketball, and baseball. (Yes, we had some talent!)

All seven of those star athletes returned the next season, along with two new kids, Bradley and Sean. Neither was very talented or athletic, but they really wanted to play football for the first time.

For my team, hard work was not only an expectation; it was in our DNA. Our work ethic had been ingrained through many years of playing together.

The two new kids struggled in summer camp. They struggled to meet the high standards of performance. Bradley almost quit. After I talked with Bradley's single mom, we decided he would stay the course, in hopes that the process would help him develop as a person and an athlete. My only "ask" of his mom was that she encourage him to work hard every day.

Fast-forward to mid-season. Bradley and Sean had grown from players who got on the field only because league "must play" rules required it to becoming defensive starters. Their willingness to work hard each practice proved the maxim "Hard work beats talent, when talent doesn't work hard." (Tim Notke, a high school basketball coach).[1]

The most rewarding feeling for me wasn't Bradley's and Sean's growth into a starting role (although that was cool to see, given how much they improved). It was the personal transformation and growth these kids experienced through consistent hard work, work that yielded a new self-confidence, focus, and presence. Bradley's mom noted that he was a different person at home and school as well as on the field. *He activated a superpower, a work ethic that enabled him to reach his next level of greatness and prove to himself that he could achieve anything he set his heart on.*

Sports will provide hundreds of hours in which a young athlete can make hard work a personal value, and a habit. Sports help establish the truth that hard work and maximum effort are the standard for *anything* one does in life. Let's show our kids that work ethic is a choice. It can become a personal belief that enables them to live in their greatness as a person, student, athlete, online gamer, musician, or whatever role they pursue. The ability to work hard doesn't reside in

> **The most rewarding feeling for me wasn't Bradley's and Sean's growth into a starting role. It was the personal transformation and growth these kids experienced through consistent hard work, work that yielded a new self-confidence, focus, and presence.**

the jersey. It's not a perk of being on a team. It flows like a river inside of them. As parents, we can uphold this standard in our kids' studies, household chores, spiritual growth, and so on.

I intentionally ingrained this belief in my two sons by buying a lawn mower when we moved to College Station, Texas, during their middle school years. I wanted them to apply the same work ethic that made them successful athletes into stewarding our home by doing chores. I intentionally wanted to disarm this generation's handicapping belief in entitlement. Instead, I went "old school" by empowering beliefs in work ethic and pride of ownership. Also, I wanted to build their mental toughness in the unrelenting Texas heat and humidity.

Work ethic is a Guidry family multigenerational characteristic. It's one of our hallmarks. It was passed down from my father, Edward "Ace" Guidry, and his father, Papa Carlton. It was honed in the southern country fields of Lafayette, Louisiana. I wasn't going to break that cycle! What can you do to intentionally teach your child(ren) some old-school life values, such as work ethic? Embrace the Warrior Parent Mentality, and apply proven proverbs, like "Train up a child in the way he should go, and when he is old he will not depart from it." (Proverbs 22:6 NKJV)

> "Hard work beats talent, when talent doesn't work hard."
>
> —TIM NOTKE

Work ethic is a life skill that will pierce through life's storms and fears. It will shatter those limiting ceilings. It will separate our kids from the competition and empower them to pursue their highest ambitions. As kids mature, you can guide them on how to channel their work ethic so that they can learn to "work smarter" while still working hard. In addition, I encourage you to model work ethic to your children. Let them see how it has made you successful in your own life. Help them embrace the truth that "Greatness is earned, not given" (J.J. Watt).[2]

SUMMARY

1. Work ethic is a belief that hard work and diligence have moral benefit.

2. Hard work will improve every area of your child's life and enhance their self-confidence, focus, presence, and competitive drive.

3. Be intentional about developing a work ethic outside of sports. Make it a value your child owns personally.

4. Make hard work the standard in your house, a value synonymous with your family name.

5. Work ethic will slay the entitlement thief and create a bridge from where kids are to what they want to accomplish.

ACTIONABLE DEVELOPMENT

» Which activities (beyond sports) can you provide for your child that will help develop a work ethic and hold them accountable to the same standards exemplified in athletics?

» Show them YouTube video clips of athletes working hard or entrepreneurs who worked hard building the companies behind their favorite apps or websites.

» Find a volunteer opportunity that enables your child to work hard serving others. For example, help clean the gym after a practice or game or do some yard work for an elderly neighbor.

» If applicable, ask an older daughter or son to show a younger sibling how to work hard at home or in sports.

PERSONAL APPLICATION

Affirmation:

» Affirm who kids are and what they are capable of. Assure them that they matter as they grow into their own personal work ethic.

» Affirm how your child is "living in their greatness" by working hard. Show them how their hard work is benefiting others.

Acknowledge:

» The hard work your child is putting in, regardless of the outcome

» Hard work must be prominent on the scorecard of their life, above any athletic stats or metrics.

Reward:

» Celebrate their hard work and growth. Praise them, and give tangible rewards.

10

THE GROWTH MINDSET

"Growth and comfort do not coexist."

—GINNI ROMETTY

"**BEST** Is the Standard."

"Win the Day."

"Play Like a Champion!"

"All In!"

Athletic programs plaster a variety of slogans or inspirational messages on the walls of their facilities, or on T-shirts. While the messages vary, the intent is clear: to influence the minds of their athletes and help them grow into their best selves.

Programs want their athletes to give their best in the weight room, on the court, on the field, during conditioning, and, most importantly, on game day. That doesn't happen without a growth mindset.

That's pretty clear and straightforward for the athlete, but what's the banner or inspirational message for the *person*?

As a parent, what sign would you post on the walls of your home?

In sports, the commitment to growth and improvement is necessary (and expected) if you want to play and succeed. This is why teams practice: to facilitate growth for each individual and for the team collectively.

That's why it's odd that in the "Champions of Life" league, most people don't choose and commit to personal growth. They don't position themselves to thrive on life's important "game days."

I believe people can achieve anything if they are willing to grow personally and work hard toward mastery in their field.

With that in mind, let's understand that children are malleable, so we parents have the opportunity to make a growth mindset a daily choice in their lives.

ESPN's "Last Dance" documentary series showed us how even NBA legend Michael Jordan had to improve his game, by adding muscle, getting stronger, trusting his teammates more, and learning a new offensive system. Think about that: A league MVP, defensive player of the year, and scoring champion knew he had to keep growing.

Or, consider the story of Lisa Fernandez, the UCLA softball legend and three-time USA Olympic gold-medal winner. Like Jordan, Fernandez continually improved upon the little things, developing her game with passion, grit, and work ethic.

Los Angeles Lakers legend Magic Johnson is a great example of an athlete applying the growth mindset (honed by leading his team to five NBA championships) to his post-basketball career as an entrepreneur. Johnson is involved with more than 20 companies and is also a tireless philanthropist. By the way, he is earning more money now than he did as an NBA star.

These examples show how a growth mindset is vital to being your best and achieving your life goals.

> **Warrior Parents don't raise children who want to sit on the sidelines of life. We craft arrows that soar and land at their target destination.**

It is important to note here that the successes above have more to do with mindset than with talent. Ninety-five percent of Fortune 500 CEOs are former athletes. And 94 percent of female "C-Suite" executives are former athletes. (Fifty-two percent of these execs played at the college level.) [1] Why do we see numbers like this? Because climbing the ladder of success in life requires a growth mindset, and sports are a great way to build this mindset. There is greatness in each of our children; sports and intentional parenting can help unleash that greatness.

Our young athletes can learn leadership, communication, critical thinking, problem-solving, and creativity through volleyball, lacrosse, swimming, wrestling, track, etc. Later in life, they can put those traits to work in their professional and personal lives.

As Warrior Parents, we are charged with being our kids' life coaches and "person" trainers. We need to apply the sports growth mindset to our kids' personal development journey and help them become the best version of themselves every day.

This mission requires us to be intentional as we help our kids be more effective in their academics, home life, and personal growth. And we should be willing to grow right along with them.

Tomorrow is not promised to any of us, so we all need to "practice how we want to play on game day!"

As our kids mature, our goal should be for them to increase their levels of self-awareness and personal accountability. We should set the same goal for ourselves. After all, the standard is the standard for *everyone.*

The WP3 sports program (detailed at the end of this book) provides a format, structure, and metrics-based goals to help you facilitate improvement through a daily 15-minute commitment to working on life skills with your child.

One of the biggest obstacles to growth is comfort (or complacency). A little success can tempt any of us to believe we have "arrived." We can live the rest of our lives on cruise control.

IBM Executive Chairman Ginni Rometty addressed this temptation, saying, "I learned to always take on things I'd never done before. Growth and comfort do not coexist." [2] We need to encourage our children to emulate people like Rometty, while also providing them lots of grace as they try new things and fail, or fall short. This grace should spring from the fact that we value our kids for who they are, more than for what they do. This is something we should affirm every day. When a kid is valued, he or she will understand this truth: "I might have failed this time, but I am not a failure!" (Or, "We lost the game, but I am not a loser.")

This distinction is vital. If a kid's identity is based solely on what is accomplished (or not accomplished) on the court or field, the sense of self-worth will suffer extreme peaks and valleys.

I learned this hard truth from 18 years of playing competitive sports. I remember the pressure of feeling that one of the only ways for me to earn love was to perform athletically. To win and keep on winning. Over time, that pressure became a crippling burden. I wondered how I would find love and affirmation when my sports career was over.

Now, I am not saying we should fail to celebrate victories and enjoy accomplishments, such as a new PR(personal record) in the weight room, on the track, or in the pool. By all means, we should reward achievement. We should also celebrate progress for its own sake.

However, the Warrior Parent Mentality doesn't get caught up in the hype. Warrior Parents and their young athletes realize that another battle always lies ahead. There is always another mountain to climb.

Warrior Parents don't raise children who want to sit on the sidelines of life. We craft arrows that soar and land at their target destination.

The beauty of the growth mindset is how it can enhance all facets of life: relationships, academics, communication, faith, sports, online activities, hobbies, career preparation, and so much more. This mindset is most effective when your child's friends or teammates share a growth journey together and keep each other accountable. As the proverb states, "As iron sharpens iron, so one person sharpens another." (Proverbs 27:17 NIV)

I'm excited to hear how you and your child are progressing as you apply the growth mindset to the journey of life. (See my contact information at the back of the book if you'd like to share.)

SUMMARY

1. A growth mindset is a lifelong process of continual personal growth and transformation: mentally, physically, spiritually, and emotionally.

2. Sports coaches intentionally facilitate continual improvement. Parents are "life coaches" for their children, with the same responsibility for the game of life.

3. Celebrate kids' progress, accomplishments, and victories, but don't rest there too long. "Growth and comfort do not coexist."

ACTIONABLE DEVELOPMENT

» Designate time daily for your child to spend growing in some area of his or her life.

» Periodically designate time for them to visualize what that target goal or aspiration looks like.

» What "stretch goal" can you create or encourage your child to pursue? (By definition, some stretch goals will not be realized, but a kid can still learn and grow from the experience.)

PERSONAL APPLICATION

Affirmation:

» As they practice a growth mindset, double down on affirming who your kids truly are—and what they are capable of—regardless of the results of any single game, match, or season.

Acknowledge:

» Mirror to your child the growth in specific areas. Help them see the progress that has been made.

» Acknowledge their commitment and effort in continual growth.

Reward:

» The willingness to fail while pursuing a stretch goal or ambition. And reward the commitment to learn and grow from a challenging experience.

» Progress! Progress! Progress!

11

THE SECRET OF TRUE
SELF-CONFIDENCE

*"I am the master of my fate:
I am the captain of my soul."*

—WILLIAM ERNEST HENLEY[1]

INTENTIONALLY practice, deliberately practice, and practice some more. It's foundational to any sport. You practice taking the shot, swinging the bat, spiking the ball, turning that double play, hitting the puck, and making that buzzer-beating 3-pointer.

Sports teach us that consistent repetition allows us to be confident and competent in our craft. A sport provides a clear transformational platform that proves how persistent mental and physical repetition (during practice, training sessions, and competitions) enables an athlete to develop true confidence.

If you have a child in sports, even for a short time, I hope you have seen his or her self-confidence improve. (If not, is it time to consider a different sport or activity?)

Self-confidence should be an organic by-product of participation in sports. And confidence shouldn't be based on talent or personality. I like how speaker and author Mel Robbins describes it: "Confidence is not a state. It's not a feeling. And it's definitely not a personality trait. Confidence is the willingness to listen to yourself, to believe in your instincts, and to trust your inner wisdom. It's the skill of believing in and listening to yourself. *Confidence doesn't just occur. It's a skill, one that's built through repeated acts of everyday courage.*"

The mental repetition of "believe in and listen to yourself" is exercised over and over again in athletics. And athletes not only try new things, they do it in front of an audience week after week. That takes self-confidence and courage, and we need to remind our kids of this fact. And we parents need to appreciate it as well!

There is a blueprint for building self-confidence that we can learn from sports and carry over into further developing the person beyond the uniform (the student, the friend, the class leader, the part-time worker, and so on).

However, before we study this blueprint, we need to tackle some myths about athletes and self-confidence.

Myth #1: Athletic confidence will automatically transfer to other areas of life. Even a very young athlete's identity can be so driven by sport that he or she doesn't develop as a whole person. Once the uniform is off, the value of the person is in question. Highly successful athletes are at high risk here, given how our culture idolizes sports stars. They are the social media icons, they are rich, and they receive all kinds of privileges and perks. Their value is built on what they do, not who they are. In the WP3 sports program, I attempt to mitigate this risk by equipping parents with a weekly "playsheet" to be reviewed with their kids. This tool cultivates self-awareness and facilitates transferring life skills like confidence to all aspects of life.

Myth #2: Life skills (like leadership, personal growth, communication, focus, grit, work ethic, competitive drive, and teamwork) that are developed through hours and hours of sports repetition will automatically apply to other areas of their life. This is *not* an automatic process. It takes intentional work by parents and other mature adults to make the transfer complete, to ensure that kids take ownership for their personal development.

We can see two different outcomes when we see how athletes apply their skills and discipline to their personal lives. As I noted earlier, 95 percent of Fortune 500 CEOs and 94 percent of female C-suite executives played competitive sports. Conversely, about 60 percent of NBA players go broke (filing for bankruptcy) within five years of retirement. And 78 percent of NFL players experience a similar fate, just two years after retiring.[3] Clearly, the sports-to-life transfer must be facilitated. It doesn't happen automatically. To facilitate this transfer, we offer a WP3 Live in Greatness mobile app that will help parents influence their kids' growth and life habits.

Myth #3: Everyone who participates in sports should receive a participation trophy. The "participation trophy" concept does not reflect the competitive nature of the real world. Yes, young athletes should be commended for completing a season, but the focus should be on developing life skills throughout that season. That development is what truly enables a young athlete to feel more confident in his or her abilities, and it provides the courage to take on new challenges and see them through.

Myth #4: Specializing in one sport will give you a competitive advantage over multisport athletes. I think there is value in specializing if you play an individual sport like golf, swimming, gymnastics, or tennis. However, team sports have so many benefits that force athletes to move, think, problem-solve, compete, communicate, play in space, and find ways to be competitive differently. I believe it enhances their overall athletic ability, intangibles, and mental capacity. Many college coaches, like Nick Saban, Dabo Swinneyy, and others, are on record about the value of athletes playing multiple sports, and their recruiting classes reflect it. (For more on the benefits of kids playing multiple sports, see https://www.usabdevelops.com/USAB/Blog/Benefits_Playing_Multiple_Sports.aspx.)

With those myths dispelled, let's examine the specifics of developing self-confidence in our kids. I will use club soccer and travel softball as the sports of reference here. Parents, as you read, envision yourselves as coach and trainer.

1. **PLAN**: Coaches/Trainers (CTs) should work to understand their players' skill levels and personalities so that they can develop practice plans that include fundamentals, skill development, game plans, and situation-specific strategies. Likewise, parents, our personal development plans for our kids should be equally intentional—based on family values, social behavior, a kid's maturity level and personal traits, and so on.

2. **TEACH**: CTs should teach their players in various ways so that they can learn and understand what, why, how, when, and where to increase awareness and ownership of a skill or scheme:

» **Auditory** – verbally explain a new penalty-kick technique or batting stance.

» **Visual** – show them how to do it. Demonstrate a new dribbling technique or way to lay down a bunt.

» **Kinesthetic** – have them do it. ("Now it's *your* turn to swing the bat!")

Parents, it's important to note that auditory-only teaching is not as effective as including visual teaching. It's more effective to model what you teach. The old adage, "Do as I say, not as I do" doesn't apply to most areas of life. Self-confidence will grow through consistent repetition: listening, seeing, and, especially, *doing* the life skills.

1. **Affirm & Acknowledge & Assist (AAA):**

   » Affirm their character, what they are capable of, and how they matter to the team. Plant the seeds for positive thoughts and self-talk.

   » Acknowledge their work ethic, effort, focus, progress, and so on.

   » Assist them in improving their craft, making corrections, building a growth mindset, adopting visualization exercises, and building self-confidence.

2. **Create Space**: Give kids freedom to try and fail toward growth as they build their self-confidence. Don't limit growth with destructive criticism. Your words will heavily influence their experience. Parents, this is vital to your child's self-confidence. The growth space you provide and the power of your words will either build or erode a kid's personal development. Remember how a Sequoia's acre-wide roots provide the foundation for its legendary growth.

3. **Go Live**: CTs let their players be free on game day. Free to express the fullness of their training and abilities. Remember that Navy SEAL maxim: "In battle you don't rise to the occasion; you sink to the level of your training." Parents, have confidence in the training you've invested in your child when they leave the house. And remember that parenting is a marathon, not a sprint, so adopt a parental growth mindset similar to Joshua Medcalf's: "Anything that happens to me today is in my best interest; it's an opportunity to learn and grow." [4]

What does the development of a life skill look like in real life? Here's a story to illustrate: I have a friend named Todd who lives in Utah. His son, James, is involved in sports and a variety of other activities. Todd decided he wanted James to learn stage presence and become a better communicator. James was in 5th or 6th grade at the time, and Todd decided to teach his son how to introduce himself to adults in social settings and engage in a conversation. After weeks of role playing at home, James was ready to go live—at a big-league baseball game in Southern California. During batting practice, James introduced himself to a man in a suit near the dugout. The man, a team executive, was so impressed by the kid's self-confidence, tone of voice, firm handshake, and eye contact that he provided a seat upgrade and a gift. Needless to say, James's dad was extremely proud. The lesson here is that Todd went through specific steps with his son. He created the space to grow, and this "Go live" experience was a success. Parents, now the ball is in your court. How will you invest in your most prized possession: your child?

> **Parenting is about persistence, patience, and love. And then more persistence."**

Self-confidence begins with you! You have the power to build your child's self-confidence through sports, and to help them bring that confidence into their personal lives. Identify and edify the little things you see your kids doing right, in athletics, at home, and in the classroom. (Focus on things that might not show up on a report card or game grade.) Affirm them in who they are, what they are capable of, and how they matter. Encourage them daily to have positive thoughts and self-talk. In his book *The Power of Self-Confidence*, Brian Tracy reminds us that "what you habitually think about eventually becomes a part of your character. Therefore, persistently think thoughts that are consistent with the kind of person you would like to be." [5] If we want our kids to see the glass as half-full, we need to help them make the mental adjustments that will grow their self-confidence.

One of the mental adjustments I instituted to grow my son's self-confidence in both high school and college football (I highly recommend starting at the youth level if possible), was a methodology I call P.L.I.O. The term stands for:

P – positive things you did well at practice and game day (10 different things)

L – learned new today at practice and game day (2 things)

I – an improvement you can make from practice and game day (1 thing)

O – ownership (how did you get 1% better today)

Utilizing P.L.I.O.'s over the years has been invaluable by empowering my kids to identify and own all the positive actions they exemplify on the field. It has narrowed their focus toward learning and growth on the path of mastering their craft in small progress-based increments. It's built and reinforced their self-confidence.

In addition, P.L.I.O.'s helps keep the sports experience in proper perspective to counter negative self-talk and the overly critical nature of some coaches (and some parents) that can stifle our kid's self-confidence overshadowing the fun and love of sports. By staying consistent in practicing P.L.I.O.'s at home you're cultivating self-awareness, ownership of their growth, and an accountability mechanism that is measurable toward whatever goals or ambitions they hope to achieve.

A warrior is confident in battle due to extensive training. Confidence, however, doesn't remove life's true threats and dangers. Children will face opposition, via social media, peer pressure, bullying, the comparison thief, fear of rejection, etc. That's why I challenge you to take on the Warrior Parent Mentality and raise a self-confident child. Use sports or any competitive activity to fan into flames their self-confidence. Empower them to soar toward living in their greatness.

Parenting is about persistence, patience, and love. And then more persistence. Building self-confidence is a marathon, not a sprint, so do not get discouraged. An infinity pool of self-confidence takes time to fill. And once full, it takes more input to *keep* it that way. Evaporation will happen. Life will happen, so keep that "living water" pouring into their pool. Remind them their value comes from who they are. A $100 bill retains its value whether it falls onto the ground, drops into water, or even suffers a slight tear. Parents, let's protect and uphold our kids' value at all costs. Let's deposit love into their account frequently. Each child is special, one of a kind, and wonderfully made, made to share their personal powers with the world.

SUMMARY

1. Self-confidence is a skill that is developed by repeatedly acting upon a thought or belief in one's powers and abilities to accomplish a task

2. Don't let sports myths create illusions about your child. Do the work to develop their self-confidence *outside* the uniform.

3. Parents, be your kids' life coach. Use the proven sports methods of development: Plan, teach, AAA (Affirm/ Acknowledge/Assist), create space, and go live.

4. Be aware of the opposing forces that will attack your child's self-confidence, so that you can empower him or her to overcome obstacles and thrive.

ACTIONABLE DEVELOPMENT

» Help them create and speak and/or listen to affirmations daily: "I am confident. I am valuable. I am worth it. I am powerful." Such affirmations will influence their thoughts and improve their self-talk.

» Help them see what a self-confident version of themselves looks like. Work through any barriers and build a bridge to becoming that self-confident person.

» Discuss how they can handle challenges to their sense of self-worth—at school, on social media, at practice, at home with siblings, at a part-time job, and so on.

PERSONAL APPLICATION

Affirmation:

» What are ways can you affirm who your kids are, what they are capable of, and that they matter as they exhibit self-confidence?

» Speak words of life and encouragement to your kids, all along the journey of living in their greatness.

Acknowledge:

» Highlight their growth and progress in daily activities. Remind them that taking action is the target. Focus on action over outcome.

» How can you role-play with your child to neutralize fearful thoughts and to help them act with confidence?

Reward:

» Celebrate their repeated ability to try.

SECTION THREE

FLETCHINGS/FEATHERS AND THE FINER POINTS OF LEADERSHIP

12

LEADERSHIP:
KNOWING, GOING, AND SHOWING

*"I've learned that people will forget what you said,
people will forget what you did, but people will
never forget how you made them feel."*

—MAYA ANGELOU[1]

LEADERSHIP in sports begins with learning to consistently lead *yourself.* Effective leaders don't preach one thing to their followers but conduct themselves in a different manner. In this section, I will show you how sports develop leaders, how that correlates to children living in their greatness, and how leadership manifests itself within and beyond sports.

First, we must be clear on what leadership is and is not. Leadership expert John Maxwell explains, "A leader is one who knows the way, goes the way, and shows the way." [2] Too often, the focus of leadership is on the last component ("shows the way"), which involves guiding others. This is what many of us think of when we hear the word "leader."

However, in youth and high school sports, those first two components are the most important. As a former youth-level coach and current varsity high school football coach at Vista Murrieta High School, I can assure you that leaders are evaluated on many criteria, but there are two areas of focus. First, the tangibles, such as work ethic, punctuality, doing the right things, doing one's job, and demonstrating self-discipline. Then there are the intangibles: character, integrity, self-confidence, dependability, adaptability, focus, and so on.

Leadership, as defined by former US Navy SEAL Jocko Willink, is built upon EXTREME OWNERSHIP. He explains, "Total responsibility for failure is a difficult thing to accept, and taking ownership when things go wrong requires extraordinary humility and courage. But doing just that is an absolute necessity to learning, growing as a leader, and improving a team's performance." [3] If you have heard Willink speak, you've felt his conviction and passion for extreme ownership in leaders. For young people in their competitive sport, coaches will (or should) hold players accountable for their assignments. This cultivates ownership. Elite teams expect ownership from each other and will hold teammates accountable. Excuses are not acceptable.

Sports instills a plethora of leadership qualities and life lessons in individuals: communication skills, servanthood, empathy, ability to motivate, problem-solving, courage, discipline, sacrifice, responsibility, and adaptability. Combine a person's gifts and personality with their leadership experience and you get a recipe for a full expression of their PERSONal greatness. In sports we've seen that in six-time Super Bowl champ Tom Brady, who has led his team to 36 fourth-quarter comeback wins during his long career. [4] We saw it in Florida QB Tim Tebow's iconic speech after losing a regular season game, then leading the Gators to a national championship. We saw it in soccer star Megan Rapinoe's leadership on and off the pitch during the 2019 World Championships. All three of these athletes expressed their leadership in different ways, but they were all effective.

Earvin "Magic" Johnson delivered one of my all-time favorite sports performances in the 1980 NBA finals. Magic, then a 20-year-old rookie, had to adapt to his Laker team's losing its Hall of Fame center (and all-time leading scorer) Kareem Abdul-Jabbar to an ankle injury prior to Game 6. Magic is arguably the greatest point guard to play basketball, but these finals revealed that he was an even greater team leader, especially in high-pressure situations.

It's important to note that Magic's leadership transcended what he did on the court. Consider, for example, what he did on the night before Game 6.

On the team's chartered plane, Magic sat in Jabbar's front-row seat. (Jabbar's injury prevented him from traveling with the Lakers.) As each teammate boarded the plane, Magic stopped him and said, "Never fear; EJ is here." He inspired his teammates with his confidence—and his million-dollar smile.

On game night, he started at center (Kareem's position). During the course of Game 6, he played all five positions as he led the team to a historic victory. He scored 42 points, grabbed 15 rebounds, and dished out 7 assists. More importantly, he took extreme ownership and led his team through adapting, communicating, inspiring confidence, and sacrificing his point guard role. Throughout the game, he displayed an intense work ethic, poise under pressure, and unparalleled passion and grit. From the time Jabbar was declared unable to play in Game 6 to the final buzzer that announced the Lakers as world champs, Magic exemplified this John Maxwell proverb: "Leaders become great, not because of their power, but because of their ability to empower others." [5] That is the "Magic" of leadership.

I emphasize that Magic, Megan, Tim, and Tom weren't born to be great leaders. Their leadership was forged in adversity, and it grew over time in the "laboratory," where parents, coaches, and teachers instilled good values. These athletes allowed life's circumstances to teach them important lessons. They invested hundreds of hours into grueling training sessions. They set goals and failed to reach some of them, but that adversity helped them develop a growth mindset. Most important, they *owned* who they are, what they are capable of, and how much they matter.

When you empower your child to live in their own greatness, it will be distinctively expressed in their own unique way, because each young athlete is one of a kind. Let's remember that as we love our kids and teach them to lead.

My daughter, Kailah, grew up with competitive brothers (two and three years older than she). They were leaders, and they helped shape her personality and develop her leadership style. For example, when I coached her in soccer for two years (as a 5- and 6-year-old: shout out to the Purple Princesses), she volunteered to lead every drill. She chased every ball with vigor. She encouraged the other girls on her team, in practices and games. (I'm not sure if she learned more from watching her brothers compete in soccer, or from them always stealing the ball from her when they played informally together.) Whatever the case, when Kailah began organized soccer, she felt like it was *her time.*

Fast-forward to a 5th-grade report card. Kailah's teacher noted she had a "BIG personality," adding that as she grew and matured, she would become a successful leader. That teacher recognized that Kailah's strong personality and ability to influence others in the classroom (coupled with high academic achievement) created a combination that spelled LEADER.

I believe that all children have the potential to be leaders, whether in sports, at school, in social settings, or at home. So let's encourage them to "know the way, go the way and show the way" for others. Let's model good leadership for them.

How does leadership correlate to your child living in greatness? Living in greatness is walking in the highest quality of *you*. It's the fullest expression of what makes you unique. Leadership is a quality, a skill that can be an extension or demonstration of PERSONal greatness. Living in greatness is not a destination. There's not necessarily a right way or wrong way. Greatness should be a *personal* standard that inspires the best version of you in each moment. True leadership equips the human spirit to serve and lead others toward a common goal.

Leadership empowers and inspires others to contribute their best for the team, on the way to a common goal. For some, that's being quiet and performing at a high level. (There are strong, silent leaders who are very effective.)

For others, it's verbally motivating one's teammates, helping them adapt to situations and make real-time adjustments.

Developing your child's leadership ability is a focus of the *Warrior Parent Playbook*. Kids will need this ability to soar in the world they live in now, and the one that awaits them later in life. You've already begun the process. You have placed your child in one of the best life and leadership education systems in the world: competitive sports. And you are reading a book that will help you make sports successful for him or her.

I encourage you: Give kids the freedom to stumble, fail, and learn from mistakes along the way. As we develop young leaders, growth and confidence are the key, not wins and losses. Young people fear being leaders for the same reason they fear so many other endeavors: the possibility of failure. Fear of failure is a common obstacle, so be ready to neutralize and restore confidence in "personal power." I love how Will Smith describes fear in the film *After Earth*: "Fear is not real. The only place that fear can exist is in our thoughts of the future. It is a product of our imagination, causing us to fear things that do not at present and may not ever exist. That is near insanity. Do not misunderstand me; danger is very real, but fear is a choice."

WP3 helps neutralize fear by allowing children to cultivate leadership with their teammates and identify opportunities to lead in their sport(s), as well as in their personal lives. This gives them the freedom to stumble and learn along with their teammates as they grow on the journey together.

The last component of developing leadership in your child is modeling it. The best way to lead is to show how it's done. And I'm not talking about getting all super-intellectual about leadership. It's as simple as explaining to your kids how you are going to work each day, providing food and shelter, paying bills, and so on is leading your family. If you are a stay-at-home mom or dad, explain how you show leadership by managing a household, setting schedules, and preparing meals. In both of the above scenarios, a parent is leading by "serving others toward a common goal."

As we develop young leaders, growth and confidence are the key, not wins and losses.

My amazing wife, Dr. MamaKai, was a phenomenal stay-at-home mom, raising our three kids and building a solid foundation for them for 14 years. Then she chose an "easier" career path: She became an internal-medicine physician. In both roles, she modeled leadership for our children and inspired each of them to be great in his or her life.

The bottom line here? Write your own story with your family. Use sports to help you develop leadership in your children as they pursue their own personal greatness. I am here to help parents transfer all that can be learned from sports to the person under the uniform. *Let's not leave sports' best lessons on the field.*

SUMMARY

1. Leadership is the ability to direct others toward a common goal. That begins with leading yourself. Sports is a wonderful platform for growing leaders.

2. Leadership involves many different qualities, including extreme ownership, adaptability, communication, humility, integrity, vision, persuasion, accountability, and confidence. Your child's personality, specific gifts, and experiences as an athlete will help form their unique leadership style.

3. Leaders are developed, not born. This life skill comes through growth, so we need to provide our kids time—and the space to fail and learn from their mistakes.

4. Model it. Show your child how you and others in your family exemplify leadership.

ACTIONABLE DEVELOPMENT

» Watch videos of athletes or movie characters who display leadership. Identify key attributes as you see them on-screen. Talk to your child and discuss how these traits can be applied to his or her daily life.

» Give kids a chance to lead at home. Put them in charge of cleanup after a party or large gathering. Ask them to plan a family game night or movie night. Opportunities like this help a kid learn and grow in a safe environment.

» Create a list of leadership qualities and review it with your child. Highlight traits that are already apparent and make a plan for developing the others.

PERSONAL APPLICATION

Affirmation:
   » Remind your child of who they are, what they are capable of, and how much they matter *daily* as they grow in leadership.

   » Speak words of life to affirm the leadership qualities you see them display (things like communication, empowering others, humility, taking initiative, empathy, integrity, vision, and confidence).

Acknowledge:
   » Recognize leadership-related effort and growth. Highlight even the little things (like speaking up during a family discussion). These are stepping-stones to larger leadership responsibilities.

   » Recognize their willingness to learn and develop their personal leadership style and operate from their strengths.

Reward:
   » Get excited and celebrate their leadership abilities. This will positively impact their lives.

   » Love on your kids. Tell them how much you love to see them play, and display leadership qualities on the court, the field, etc.

13

COMPETITIVE DRIVE

*"Do you not know that in a race all the runners run, but only one gets the prize? **Run in such a way as to get the prize.**"*

—1 CORINTHIANS 9:24 NIV

COMPETITIVE DRIVE is one of the life skills I love the most. I will explain how to develop this drive (in your child and in yourself), but first I want to share a story about a competitively driven person.

Kobe Bryant was one of the most competitively driven athletes of his era. His nickname, "The Black Mamba," reflected his fierce mentality and competitive fire. He received many accolades during his Hall of Fame career (for his athletic ability, work ethic, and court awareness), but what drove him was his desire to always be the best version of himself. (I hope this phrase rings a bell for you.)

Upon retirement, Bryant wrote children's books about the journey to become the best version of oneself.

Competitive drive is a potent life skill because it applies to so many situations and circumstances—as long as your objective holds personal significance for you. It has to mean something.

For example, the 2008 USA Basketball squad was labeled the "Redeem Team," after the Americans failed to win the gold medal at the 2004 Olympics.

The team's coaches summoned the country's best NBA players, including LeBron James, Dwyane Wade, Carmelo Anthony, Chris Paul, and Kobe Bryant. The mission was clear: return the USA to Olympic basketball dominance. All of the players were on board, but Bryant's competitive drive helped him stand out, even among a roster of legendary talent. This drive was evident in training, practices, and games. I like how sports journalist Jonathan Abrams described it: "What the Redeem Team did in 2008 remains the standard, and largely because of Bryant. He was able to be an alpha dog on a team of alpha dogs."[1] Bryant's drive was especially evident in the Americans' hard-fought victory over Spain (whose roster featured several NBA stars) in the gold medal game.

A strong competitive drive features three key components, components that can be applied to anyone, regardless of talent. (These components are consistently activated and cultivated in our WP3 sports program for youth and high school sports teams and other competitive activities.)

The first component? Identify a clear objective or prize, something that has meaning for your child. This sounds simple, but identifying *why* a prize is significant is vital. Significance will be the fuel to drive a young athlete when he or she doesn't feel up to the task, or when adversity strikes. Identifying the right goal will take some digging, listening, and trust-building, especially when dealing with younger children. Depending on a kid's age, the prize might be earning Dad's praise, or securing a college scholarship to create a better life for himself and his family. For other kids, winning helps them feel valued by their peers. Whatever the prize, it must be significant to them.

The "drive" part of competitive drive is also fueled by loss aversion. (Some people are more motivated by avoiding a loss than securing a win.) This raises the age-old debate in the sports world: "Do you hate to lose more than you love to win?" I believe the former is the stronger motivator. Consider the All Blacks, the legendary New Zealand Rugby club. They believed, as author James Kerr noted, that "by setting even the most unrealistic self-expectation, the aversion to the failure of not reaching the goal is much stronger than the desire to reach it." [2]

The second component of developing a competitive drive is to continually strive for new ways to grow, to learn, and to gain a competitive advantage. This requires self-examination and self-awareness, followed by the search for new ways to improve. As a parent, you can help your child by being honest and objective. Become a mirror to your child. Be loving and age-appropriate, and don't undermine your child's confidence, but be truthful. You might need to talk to a coach for help in guiding your child to grow and improve, beyond what's being done in practice. Talk about removing barriers to development. After all, who knows your child's personality and learning style better than you? Consider watching videos of older, more accomplished athletes who play your child's position on the football field or compete in the same events in track and field, swimming, or gymnastics, etc.

Be as creative as you can, but consult the experts and build on existing knowledge and techniques. There is no need to reinvent the wheel.

Finally, helping your child develop their competitive drive requires them to be fully present in each moment, activating their mental and physical abilities toward a meaningful objective. (Many kids demonstrate this presence when they are playing a favorite video game. Note their intense focus and desire to win.) How can you encourage "gamer-like" intensity in sports or in the classroom?

> **As a parent, you can help your child by being honest and objective. Become a mirror to your child. Be loving and age-appropriate, and don't undermine your child's confidence, but be truthful.**

You might be surprised at how even very young athletes can have competitive drive.

I remember coaching the Purple Princesses, my daughter's 5- and 6-year-old soccer team. If you've coached kids this young, you know it requires monumental effort to hold their attention for anything longer than a minute.

During our practices, I would create little games to help develop their competitive drive and get them to practice with presence, power, and purpose. Once, I created two teams: The Purple and The Princesses and set a prize that all the girls could win. The competition was a relay. Each player dribbled the ball as fast as she could toward their goal, kicked it in, and ran back to tag the next girl in line. The objective was to repeat the cycle until each of the two goals was full of soccer balls. Then both teams could celebrate. The prize was a post-practice snack, but it would be awarded only if both teams gave maximum effort, cheered for each other, and followed my rules.

You probably won't be shocked to hear that all of these young girls were able to meet all three objectives. Both teams were winners, and these kids unknowingly developed a new level of competitive drive. They earned their fruit snacks. Even young kids can summon competitive drive, given the right motivation, by being fully present and having a meaningful objective.

Of course, building drive will take intentional work. We must encourage accountability and daily work toward the objective.

If you follow sports at all, you've probably seen athletes who write something significant or motivating on their shoes, wristbands, or socks. (An older athlete might get a tattoo.) This is part of competitive drive. Visual symbols or cues help remind us of our values and sources for motivation. Over time, of course, an athlete might rely less on symbols, as certain values and practices become automatic.

THE WARRIOR MENTALITY

Competitive drive is cultivated when we place significance on doing the little things right. In football, for example, for one offensive play to work, 11 athletes have to do their jobs. The offensive line has to know the snap count and the individual blocking assignments. The wide receivers and tight ends have to run the correct routes and block the right defensive backs (often assuming both tasks on a single play). The running backs have to know whether to run a pass route or stay in the back-field to protect the quarterback. The quarterback, of course, must orchestrate everything, making sure every player is in the correct position. He receives signals from the sideline, remains aware of the play clock, and notices what the defense is doing. If only one offensive lineman loses focus and misses a block, the defense can blow up the play. In football, as in other sports (and life itself), the sum of a bunch of little things done right produces a positive outcome.

So parents, let's discover how our kids are competitively driven, and let's transfer those elements into their sports, academics, and life in general. Remember, the little things add up.

Let's face it: Competition is woven into our culture. That's why the ability to embrace a challenge and the drive to be at one's best will position your child for success in life. Sports is a transformational platform to awaken and nurture the competitive drive in your child, a drive he or she will need to soar in life.

SUMMARY

1. Competitive drive is a valuable skill. This drive is based on having a meaningful objective and consciously striving to achieve it.

2. Competitive drive requires:
   a. Continued growth, learning, self-discipline, and developing a work eethic to gain a competitive advantage.
   b. Practicing presence and power toward one's purpose, with intentional reminders along the way.
   c. Winning in the little things.

3. Competitive drive isn't about the opponent; it's about your drive to be the best version of yourself. In the big picture, we are truly competing against the person we saw in the mirror yesterday.

4. This drive is the same, regardless of how big the goal or opponent. Give your child the freedom to fail on his or her quest toward personal greatness.

ACTIONABLE DEVELOPMENT

» What are some of the "little things" that you can challenge your child to do better? Is it household chores, drills at practice, homework, or consistently doing their P.L.I.O.'s after practices and games?

» Spend time with your kids and help them identify goals or dreams. (Does your child want to make the honor roll, earn a scholarship, or learn a new position in his or her sport?) Discuss what it would feel like to achieve the goals. Maybe your child's biggest dreams lie beyond sports. Maybe he or she wants to design video games or play eSports. Whatever the case, spend time discussing the consistent drive and sacrifices required. Create or buy visual cues or motivators (like posters, photographs, or paintings) and display them in a bedroom, workout area, or other prominent place.

PERSONAL APPLICATION

Affirmation:

» Let's remind our kids who they are, what they are capable of, and that they matter!

» Get them to speak their target or goal and their "why." Affirm their drive and mental and physical skills and effort, regardless of the outcome.

Acknowledge:

» Highlight all the good things a kid does. Note improvement.

» Point out how your child's effort is paying off. Progress creates momentum!

Reward:

» Remind them how you love to watch them play and compete.
» Celebrate their victories in the little things. Years of coaching have taught me that the average athlete does 5 to 7 things right for every mistake he or she makes.

14

PLAYING WITH PASSION

"I have no special talents.
I am only passionately curious."

—ALBERT EINSTEIN [1]

IN THE 2017 NBA finals, LeBron James became the first player in league history to average a triple double (33 points, 12 rebounds and 10 assists per game). He played with relentless effort, even though he rarely left the court for a breather. Despite his Cleveland team being overmatched (by the Golden State Warriors), LBJ played with an intensity and fire that heightened all his other abilities to superhero levels.

What ignited this fire? What amplified his confidence, competitive drive, grit, focus, and work ethic each night? It's a one-word answer: PASSION.

Passion is the life skill that heightens or amplifies all the other life skills in the arrow. Passion is the element that fuels everything else, enabling an athlete to get the most from his or her abilities and preparation. Passion ignites our mental focus. It injects vitality into a person, a project, or a vision.

Human beings are not designed to be robots; we are designed to feel, to care, to love, and to live lives of meaning. Passion does all of this, and more. But how do we awaken passion in our kids? Angela Duckworth, author of *Grit: The Power of Passion and Perseverance*, observes, "A passion is developed more than it is discovered. In other words, it takes time and experience and encouragement to be able to say, one day, 'I have a calling.'" [2]

In sports, coaches are always trying to ignite passion in their players, inspiring the best in them. Coaches use inspirational movies, motivational speeches, team-building exercises, and more. Coaches know passion has the potential to take their players to a new level, and it can become contagious, transforming an average individual or team to elite status.

THE WARRIOR PARENT MENTALITY

How do you develop passion in your child? One method is to observe and journal what excites or motivates your child. Which movies, video games, books, or websites captivate and inspire them? Is there a theme you can discern? What resonates with your child?

Also, pay close attention to how your kid plays and practices. What brings out his or her passion? Is it when an opposing player "pushes their buttons," or when a referee or umpire does something "unjust"? Or is it when the team is losing and your child has a chance to be a hero?

If we are "present" and observant, we will learn something. For example, Deion "Prime Time" Sanders shared how seeing his single mother struggle during his childhood ignited his passion for sports. He wanted to provide a better life for her, and for all of his family. That led him to excel in two sports. He was very good in baseball, but a Hall of Fame NFL player (arguably the greatest cornerback to play the game).

As a child, Oprah Winfrey vowed she wasn't going to be a maidservant like her grandmother. Her passion and perseverance drove her to become a media mogul and best-selling author, as well as a philanthropist.

> 66
>
> **I remind my kids all the time, "You are one-of-a kind, and the world will be a better place with a passionate version of you in it."**

So, fan into flames your child's passion, even before they are able to participate in sports or any competitive activity. Cultivating passion will enhance a child's confidence, focus, work ethic, leadership ability, personal growth, and so much more—things that will create an expression of their BEST SELF for the world to experience. I remind my kids all the time, "You are one-of-a kind, and the world will be a better place with a passionate version of you in it."

Parents, I must note that this effort is a journey, not a one-time thing. My wife has played a huge part in helping to cultivate passion in each of our children. For example, my elder son, Javelin, wasn't as focused academically during his final semester in high school (call it "senioritis"). His progress report reflected it, and his passion during track season was subsequently affected. Despite the fact he had recently signed his letter of intent to play college football on a full scholarship at the University of Utah, I was riding him pretty good about his grades. I even solicited his future University of Utah defensive backs coach, Sharrieff Shah, to verbally provide a firm Los Angeles "Dorsey Dons" nudge of encouragement to get his grades up. My wife, however, calmly spent an afternoon connecting with our son, helping him get organized and reminding him of his short- and long-term aspirations. At his next track meet, the prestigious Arcadia Invitational, he won the 100 meters in a blazing 10.34, just 17/100ths of a second off the meet record held by Noah Lyles. He jokingly reminded his parents, "See what can happen when I'm not stressed". And yes, his grades subsequently went back up. Plus, his younger siblings learned through observing this experience, and we had no additional "senioritis intervention" meetings the following two graduation years.

Remember, it is a journey of triumphs and lessons learned, with a few emotional casualties along the way. Be encouraged that you are intentionally giving your child a head start, because this will give them more time to live a life of deep conviction and passion.

SUMMARY

1. Passion is a life skill that has the ability to amplify all the other life skills that help a child live in greatness.

2. Passion can be cultivated and intentionally developed through observing your child in life's circumstances, sports scenarios, and/or in the characters and missions of their favorite movies, books, or video games.

3. Journal and fan into flames the passion in your child. See what new heights they soar to.

PERSONAL APPLICATION

Affirmation:

» How can you affirm and celebrate who your kid (or kids) are and what they are capable of? How can you show them that they matter, and so do their passions in life? Speak words of life!

Acknowledge:

» Identify and mirror back to them when they exhibit passion in their sports, at home, at school, or wherever. This builds self-awareness and helps kids take ownership of their passion.

» What's your plan to facilitate conversation after a movie or video game, as you seek to understand which character and mission resonated with your child and why? Do the work to incorporate that mission into some competitive activity. Observe them trying to emulate certain character traits, and encourage them along the way.

Reward:

» Celebrate passion when you see it.

» *Enthusiastically* remind your child that you love
to see them play with passion in their competitive
activities.

15

THE FREEDOM
OF SELF-DISCIPLINE

"Self-discipline is a form of freedom.
Freedom from laziness and lethargy, freedom from
the expectations and demands of others,
freedom from weakness and fear—and doubt."

—H.A. DORFMAN [1]

AS A CHILD'S sports career unfolds (through recreation-level sports to competition at higher levels, such as AAU or club teams), the chances to build self-discipline abound. Through my years as a coach and a parent, I have become convinced that kids have the capacity to exercise an astounding level of self-discipline as they work toward meaningful goals. And this life skill requires no talent to activate it. It's all about receiving the proper guidance and motivation toward fulfilling a meaningful purpose.

Self-discipline is a combination of training your mind and your body. As Kobe Bryant stated, "I started [working out] at 5 a.m. until 7 a.m. I could go again from 11 a.m. until 2 p.m., and from 6 p.m. until 8 p. m. By starting earlier, I set myself up for an extra workout each day. I didn't only train my body; I trained my mind too."

Bryant demonstrated how one's level of self-discipline reflects the strength of his ambition and the importance of the goal he was pursuing.

Parents, we need to understand that competitive athletics (or any competitive activity) will develop this life skill. That's why it's important to encourage our kids toward ever-higher levels of self-discipline if they want to be effective at their craft, including academics and their eventual career. For instance, we have a family friend who was extremely dedicated and disciplined in basketball. He took hundreds of shots before school and trained multiple times each day (like Kobe Bryant.)

> **Remember, modeling self-discipline is more powerful than teaching it.**

Unfortunately, a high school car accident left him unable to play basketball anymore. However, he channeled his sports-related self-discipline to a new endeavor: the online game *Fortnite*. He rose early every morning, warmed up on the sticks (video game controllers), and spent an hour or so practicing specific gaming techniques before heading to school. After school he was back on the sticks, practicing to compete with other gamers from around the world. His goal was to win tournaments and earn $75,000 from *Fortnite* within a year. Self-discipline was a key ingredient toward that meaningful objective, which he achieved.

Please note that kids might need frequent reminders about self-discipline before they are able to take ownership for themselves. Let's make sure our kids understand the "why" of self-discipline, as this will help them own it. The more a kid exercises self-discipline in life, the more it will become a habit. As Gary Keller (of Keller Williams Realty fame) observes in his book *The One Thing*, "When you discipline yourself, you're essentially training yourself to act in a specific way. Stay with this long enough and it becomes routine—in other words a habit."[3]

An important caveat here: Be mindful of your child's attitude and behavior. Is the discipline becoming too burdensome? Do you observe a consistent lack of motivation? If these signs are present, it's time to gauge if the activity is truly meaningful. Forcing kids to do too much (or too much, too soon) can cause them to burn out in sports or any activity. (For example, according to a poll from the National Alliance for Youth Sports, almost 70 percent of US kids stop playing organized sports by age 13. The reason: "It's just not fun anymore.")[4]

So, let's affirm, encourage, and celebrate our kids' self-discipline in their sports, academics, and personal life. Let's highlight the little things they do consistently, especially the helpful routines and habits they have formed. Momentum from the little things is huge when building routines and habits.

For example, compliment your kid when you see him or her doing flexibility exercises at night or doing push-ups or sit-ups on the living room floor. Or running pass patterns in the backyard. Whatever the case, be your kid's biggest supporter. Also, show them how those habits can apply to learning a musical instrument or a new language. Show how you apply self-discipline on the job or at home. Highlight the successful outcomes it has produced. Remember, modeling self-discipline is more powerful and inspiring than teaching it.

Emphasizing the significance of self-discipline will lead to routines and habits that will enable and empower your child to be the best version of him- or herself, right now and for a lifetime. Parents, we have the honor of teaching this meaningful life skill. I still remember growing up and seeing my dad wake up at 5 a.m. to go work. And every Saturday morning we knew it was clean-up time before we could play any sports. Sunday morning meant time for church. Through those routines, we understood the importance of taking care of one's family. We learned work ethic, as well as good stewardship of one's home and faith.

Parents, which disciplines will you instill in your children as you help them learn meaningful life principles? I know the global COVID-19 pandemic has forced families across the world to adopt new routines and rekindle some that had drifted away. So let's be intentional and help our kids be disciplined to live in their greatness!

SUMMARY

1. Self-discipline is an optimizing skill that has the potential and power to impact every area of your child's life. The key is to learn what motivates a kid to exercise self-discipline in his or her life.

2. Sports require and develop self-discipline, but let's remember to channel this skill toward *all* endeavors, including academics, spiritual growth, and home life.

3. Generate momentum through celebrating kids' discipline in the little things. This will help them build habits that will empower them to be their best selves.

4. Keep the lines of communication open and active to help kids grow as athletes. At the same time, recognize when a sport (or any activity) is no longer meaningful or fun. Then be willing to take whatever corrective measures are necessary.

ACTIONABLE DEVELOPMENT

» Ask your coach how your son or daughter can become more effective in their sport. Which drills or activities can help achieve this goal?

» What family disciplines or routines can you create that reflect the life principles or values that are important in your household?

» What can you model in your own life? How can you help your child see the positive outcomes that self-discipline produces?

PERSONAL APPLICATION

Affirmation:

>> How can you affirm who your child is, what they are capable of, and that they matter when you see them exercising self-discipline?

>> Affirm the little things that have become routine in a kid's life (i.e., making their bed and doing other chores).

Acknowledge:

>> Mirror to them the progress and growth that self-discipline has produced.

>> Highlight all the plays that go unnoticed on the field, court, or pitch when they were self-disciplined. (For example, a player holding his tongue instead of protesting a bad call from the referee, risking a technical foul, or worse.)

Reward:

>> Celebrate your young person for who they are. Let them know how valuable they are. Say, "I see all of your hard work and personal growth."

16

ADAPTABILITY =
FLEXIBILITY + VERSATILITY

*"Adaptability combines flexibility with versatility.
Flexibility is your willingness to adapt. It's your attitude.
Versatility is your ability to adapt. It's your aptitude."*

—BO HANSON [1]

THE COVID-19 global pandemic has changed our way of life, from leaders in government, healthcare, business, and education to everyday people. The skill of adaptability is being tested; we are all being forced to exercise it. There is no "normal" way of life anymore.

Some people are struggling with all the change. But many have adapted well, choosing to see this as an opportunity to improve, learn, and grow. That is the essence of adaptability: the ability to adjust to changing conditions or circumstances. I love how adaptability is inherently integrated into sports—and can be applied to other areas of a young athlete's life.

Myron Rolle, MD, is a great example. Myron was a star football player at Florida State University who was drafted by the Tennessee Titans. He is also a Rhodes Scholar and a graduate of FSU's medical school. He is currently a neurosurgeon resident at Harvard Medical School and Massachusetts General Hospital. Yes, he went from pro athlete to neurosurgeon. During a recent interview with CNBC, he explained how football prepared him to adapt to COVID-19: "That comes from my football background, where adjustments and adaptation happen on the fly within a game. . . . You never know what the other opponent is going to throw at you, so . . . you need to be able to be flexible." [2]

Rolle chose to put himself in the game of life. He volunteered to work in the ICU to treat COVID-19 patients, demonstrating his willingness, versatility, and aptitude to serve others. Parents let's remember that sports teach adaptability and other life skills that can equip our children for whatever life may bring. It's encouraging to hear it directly from Dr. Rolle: "Football has done so much for me, given me friends, family, given me life lessons that now I can use in the operating room or just as a leader." [3]

The very nature of parenting is adaptability. The Warrior Parent Mentality embraces shifting conditions and unforeseen challenges, because children are unpredictable and curious. We parents understand the mantra "If you stay ready, you ain't gotta get ready." In other words, we must be ready to adapt and walk in presence, power, and purpose, regardless of circumstances. And we can help our kids employ adaptability in their sport(s) and in their personal lives. This is part of empowering them to live in greatness.

It's important to acknowledge that every child's personality is different. Some kids are inclined to adapt. Others, not so much. Staying aware of each child's personality will help us cultivate and nurture adaptability into his or her life.

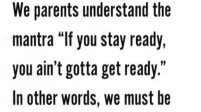

We parents understand the mantra "If you stay ready, you ain't gotta get ready." In other words, we must be ready to adapt and walk in presence, power, and purpose, regardless of circumstances.

So let's identify a few inhibitors to adaptability that can affect children (and adults too):

1. Having a rigid or closed mind. Refusing to be open to various options.

2. Being prideful. Believing that "my way is the best; I don't need anyone else's input."

3. Being fearful to take risks or color outside the lines, even when circumstances require it.

4. Lack of empathy. Some people cannot adapt as leaders because they are unable to put themselves in another's shoes or gather new information when making a decision.

5. An inability to be fully present in the moment. This can cause a person to miss key information that would enable him or her to adapt and adjust.

Parents, we can counter these inhibitors and improve our kids' adaptability. Here's how:

» Have an open mind. With an open mind, you can adjust your thought process and embrace challenges. Look for opportunities to encourage an open mind during sports. For example, when a referee makes a bad call, is your child going to sink into a funk or rise above the adversity and focus on the next play? Or, what happens when a key teammate gets injured? Do the other players give up, or do they adapt a "next man up" mentality and adjust to the challenge? A wise coach helps his or her players recalibrate their mindset to cope with change. A wise parent does the same.

» Keep learning. "Stay ready." Encourage your child to read, learn, and be curious. In times of change, we should encourage young athletes to ask questions—to seek new information and learn to process it. Humility is an important attribute here. Let's encourage our kids to stay hungry and humble, to become lifelong learners.

» Maintain a growth perspective. I encourage readers to review the chapter on "The Growth

Mindset" and apply this principle: "Anything that happens to me today is in my best interest; it's an opportunity to learn and grow." (Joshua Medcalf)

» After a game or tournament, enjoy a milk shake and some fries with your child and do a "debrief." If things did not go well on the court or the field, use the opportunity to ward off negative self-talk, which can lead to discouragement.

» Be willing to take risks. Empower your child to have the courage to act, to speak up against "the way it's always been done." This kind of courage almost always involves risk. Let's help our kids be willing to take these risks.

» Be innovative. Innovation is foundational to adaptability. Innovators are able to see things from a different perspective. Innovation seeks new ways to add value to people and circumstances. Let's raise innovators! Coaches have won Super Bowls and league championships by being innovative. They invent new plays and even entirely new offensive and defensive systems.

Parents, let's encourage adaptability in sports, at home, and at school. In the WP3 sports program, we enable young athletes to become self-aware, to take ownership, and apply adaptability everywhere. You are not alone on this journey. Other parents share your goals, and we can all learn from each other.

In closing, please remember that the best way to teach adaptability is to model it. Talk to your child about how you are adapting to changing conditions. Let them see what you are doing. I know some parents who let their kids see how they set up a "home office" to work remotely during the COVID crisis. Your personal advice and example will inspire your child.

When I decided to write this book, I explained to my kids that I was leaving corporate America to pursue my passion to impact young people and families by creating a "new normal" for youth and high school sports. I have included my kids on this journey, and the adaptations it has brought to our entire family. I've shared how a life filled with sports has prepared me to take this risk. In some ways, I forced adaptation on them, but my objective was to help them learn and grow. Although my kids are young adults now, I still encourage the Warrior Parent Mentality. It informs them and sustains them through their current challenges.

During times like the current pandemic, it is more important than ever for our kids to learn that "Those who remain flexible and have the ability to adapt their thinking and behavior to circumstances possess an important skill." (Melissa Cory, co-founder, director, and producer of the Women in Leadership Conference) [4]

I am certain that adaptability will empower your child to live in his or her own personal greatness. Let's help them lean in to this key life skill.

SUMMARY

1. Adaptability is the ability to adjust oneself to different conditions. It's a core value of sports and parenting.

2. Adaptability is learned through sports at every level, and it's applicable to all domains of life.

3. Adaptability inhibitors include a closed mind, pride, fear of risk, lack of empathy, and the inability to be fully present in each moment.

4. Adaptability accelerators include an open-minded attitude, a hunger for learning, maintaining a growth perspective, the willingness to take risks, and being innovative.

5. Model adaptability at home by letting your children see how you incorporate adaptability into various facets of everyday life.

ACTIONABLE DEVELOPMENT

» Watch an athletic contest or a favorite movie, and ask your kid(s) to identify how coaches, players, or characters adapt to various situations. When the game or movie ends, ask, "What did you learn from what we just watched?"

» How can you improve their adaptability skill at home by forcing them to take a risk or to find a new solution to an old problem or challenge? If a child is facing adversity, spend time together to discuss and explore the best solution.

Affirmation:

>> As your child seeks to become more adaptable, how can you consistently affirm who they are, what they are capable of, and how much they matter to you?

>> Set a reminder to send a periodic text message to affirm them at school, at least once a week.

Acknowledge:

>> How can you reflect to your child all the ways they demonstrated adaptability during or after a given situation—in sports, at school, or at home?

>> Point out their progress in being more adaptable. Help them see how adaptability has empowered them to live in personal greatness.

>> Recognize when they are present "in the now," activating their power and channeling it toward a purpose. Point this out, and encourage them to keep growing.

Reward:

>> Celebrate even the smallest areas of growth. This will build a kid's confidence in his or her ability to be adaptable.

>> Applaud their effort to adapt during difficult conditions. (For example, has your kid adapted well to remote learning, competing without people in the stands, or even missing a sports season?)

17

FINDING FOCUS

*"I focus on this one thing: Forgetting the past
and looking forward to what lies ahead,
I press on to reach the end of the race. . . ."*

—PHILIPPIANS 3:13-14 (NLT)

FOCUS is the ability to direct your full attention toward a moment in time. It's approaching life with a clear vision. This is an invaluable skill, and sports provide a great way to develop it. If our kids can become focused, it will benefit almost every area of their lives.

I learned a lot about focus during those days of coaching my daughter (and other young girls) in recreational youth soccer. Imagine 10 cute little girls (five on each team), chasing the soccer ball like a swarm of bees. Of course, at this age not all of the girls are interested in the ball. There's always one who is playing with the drawstring on her shorts or picking dandelions on the pitch.

However, even at this young age, there's usually one girl who is truly focused. I had a girl like this on my team. It wasn't uncommon for her to dribble the ball away from the "hive" and score five or more unassisted goals.

What made this girl stand out? What enabled her to seem so advanced? Focus. She practiced with a focus every week at a level the other girls hadn't developed yet. It wasn't anything I magically developed as a coach. Her parents told me that she simply loves soccer: "She plays it with her siblings all the time, and she wants to be good at it."

> ❝
> **Gratitude is a key focus point because it can neutralize many harmful societal obstacles to success—things like entitlement, ego, pride, and selfishness. These things can limit athletes' potential and their ability to positively impact others' lives.**

Focused athletes (like my young soccer prodigy) have the ability to block out distractions and center their attention on what is important *right now*. She had a sniper-like focus, whether we were doing a drill, scrimmaging, or competing in an official game. (However, during the down time, she was laughing and giggling like a typical five-year-old.)

Snipers spend hundreds of hours training themselves to block things out, even closing one eye to channel their full attention and vision toward their target.

Parents, we need to develop this kind of focus in our children. Sports helps young athletes develop focus through hours of games and practices, but the training we provide at home is the most important. We can accelerate growth by understanding each child's personality, learning style, and obstacles. We also need to discover the best way to motivate our kids so that focus becomes a habit.

I am confident of this: If you apply the WPM concept of Presence, Power, and Purpose, you will lift your child's focus to the next level.

The adage "Whatever you focus on, you are going to find it" is so true in life. Is your focus on the glass being half full or half empty? Children need your guidance regarding what to focus on as they develop into adulthood.

In sports, successful coaches focus on "the process," not necessarily the long-term goal. They believe if players are 100-percent committed to the process *every day*, goals (both short- and long-term) will be met. That process usually includes elements like personal growth, a strong work ethic, team bonding, grit, enjoying the moment, and, most importantly, gratitude. Gratitude is the sleeper focus point because it can neutralize many harmful societal obstacles to success—things like entitlement, ego, pride, selfishness, and so on. These things can limit athletes' potential and their ability to positively impact others' lives. Our recent global pandemic has forced us to reflect on the many things we should be grateful for, and to realize just how much of the "normal ways of life" we took for granted—including the privilege to play and watch sports.

Parents, I encourage you to regularly examine which elements of your child's personal development grab their focus. (Just as you might receive a quarterly review at work.) I intentionally wrote this book and created WP3 Sports to equip parents and enhance their focus on personally developing and empowering their children to live in greatness. This greatness will position kids to succeed in life and give parents a sense of confidence and certainty that their offspring are ready to launch and soar when they get the opportunity. Sports is a fun and proven transformational platform to contribute to the process, but our focus is larger. We are concerned about the total person. I believe parents with the Warrior Parent Mentality can help their children grow into well-rounded and successful people, in sports and beyond.

SUMMARY

1. Focus is a mental skill. Focused people are able to concentrate and center their attention on a specific activity or outcome.

2. Focus requires intentional mental training. Practicing "presence, power, and purpose" is a useful method.

3. Parents should provide guidance on identifying what to focus on in different situations. (For example, process versus outcome, personal and team growth versus winning, or enjoyment versus obligation.)

4. Focus is a skill that applies to every aspect of life. It often involves blocking out distractions. Remember: "Whatever you focus on, you're going to find it."

ACTIONABLE DEVELOPMENT

» Study and journal your child's learning style. What motivates them to focus best? What hinders their ability to focus? Use this information to create conditions for success with your child. For example, do you need to make adjustments at home to help your child be more successful at completing homework assignments or studying for a test? Also, make sure you understand your child's optimal learning style (visual, reading/writing, auditory, or kinesthetic).

» Teach and practice the importance of how eye contact, body posture, and intentional listening can help a person focus.

» List a few ways that you can model focus for your kids. Let's allow our children to see us setting a good example as focused adults.

PERSONAL APPLICATION

Affirmation:

» How can you affirm who they are, what they are capable of, and that they matter when they're demonstrating focus at home, on the field/court, at school, or in social settings?

Acknowledge:

» Let your child know when you see him or her being focused. Highlight this good behavior so that they develop self-awareness and ownership of their ability to focus.

» Call attention to the times when focus helps your child block out distractions and "nice" things" to focus on the "main thing."

Reward:

» Get excited and celebrate their ability to focus in different situations: during practice, games, at school, at home, and so on.

18

GRIT MAKES GOATS

"When I get knocked down, I'll get back up.
I may not be the smartest person in the room,
but I'll strive to be the grittiest."

—ANGELA DUCKWORTH [1]

WHEN I THINK of grit, I think of the unyielding courage and continued effort to do or achieve something of value, even in the face of difficulties, hardship, opposition, or failure. And that immediately brings to mind American gymnast Simone Biles.

When it comes to gymnastics, Simone is the GOAT. She has won 25 World Championships medals (19 of them gold), five Olympic medals (four golds), and she's created moves and skills never before seen in her sport. [2] What's more, she has a smile that can light up a whole arena.

She's talented, she's athletic, and she has a winning personality—which is a very important component of a gymnast's repertoire. However, I believe her greatest asset is her grit. What we don't see on TV during the Olympics and other competitions are the dozens of times she has fallen in practice, or failed at being the first woman to nail a double-twisting, double somersault dismount off the balance beam or perform a triple double on floor exercise (a double backflip with three twists).

Simone would eventually achieve both of these historic feats.

We didn't see the muscle pulls, the broken toes, the fractured ribs, and all the mental stress that accompany becoming (then maintaining) the honor of being the world's top female gymnast.

What's more, Simone has displayed unyielding courage as she endured seeing a parent battle substance abuse. This led to her being raised (and later adopted) by her loving grandparents.

Simone faced years of sexual abuse from a longtime USA Gymnastics physician, as well as the devastation of seeing the 2020 Tokyo Olympics postponed (and possibly canceled) due to COVID-19.

Simone's story should encourage parents to develop grit in their children through sports. This effort starts with guiding our kids to push through hardships, because that effort strengthens their character.

Grit is mental toughness. It's a spirit of perseverance that is forged through the fires of punishing practice sessions, and by pushing through mental and physical barriers. It's falling down but rising again. It's investing the effort required to master one's craft. Grit is earned, not given.

That's why we need to (wisely) push our children to remain steadfast and to be persistent as they work toward something of value. It can be hard to push our kids, but we need to realize that grit will help them later in life. The ability to live in greatness is not a gift you can deliver to a child. It must be earned. Every great success story (from Sara Blakely to Tyler Perry to Eric Thomas to Simone Biles) involves grit, grit that is refined through the fires of adversity and strengthened through consistent effort. None of these people would have made such a significant impact on the world without grit.

Grit goes hand in hand with passion. As Angela Duckworth states, "I think the misunderstanding . . . is that it's only the perseverance part that matters. But I think that the passion piece is at least as important. I mean, if you are really, really tenacious and dogged about a goal that's not meaningful to you, and not interesting to you — then that's just drudgery."[3] That's why helping our children identify what they truly value is vital in fueling the engine to persevere through difficulties, to remain hopeful in spite of setbacks and failure.

The Warrior Parent Mentality means we develop grit in young lives by encouraging our kids to get back up when they fall down or get knocked down. It's finishing what you start, with 100-percent effort. It's pursuing your goals with passion, even if the odds are against you and failure is possible, or even likely. Grit is a mentality, a character trait that can be learned at practice, games, at home, in the neighborhood, or in school.

How do we teach our kids grit? We are their life coaches. We can show them what life's trials can teach us. For example, a good basketball coach wouldn't allow a player to sulk after missing a key shot in a game, or to avoid taking such shots in the future. That would be taking the easy way out.

Conversely, a wise coach wouldn't let a "star player" develop an entitlement mindset and fail to work hard for playing time. We need to look for the same kind of teachable moments in our kids' lives beyond sports. Let's commit to adding grit to our kids' scorecards. Let's celebrate when they demonstrate unyielding courage and resolve to compete. Let's applaud the mental toughness required to try again and again and again, in pursuit of a worthy goal. Let's remind them of their greatness along the way.

By the way, Michael Jordan's mom didn't protest to the high school coach or transfer him to a different school when her son failed to make the varsity basketball team as a sophomore. (Yes, even Michael Jordan once faced this disappointment, which is common to so many athletes.) Instead, she told young MJ, "You have to work harder and get better to earn a spot on the team next season, if you really want it."

Now, that is a Warrior Parent Mentality worth celebrating!

We want to raise winners in life, based on a scorecard that measures the values that will help them develop as people and live in greatness every single day. That scorecard will look different at six or seven years old than it will when a kid hits age 12. And it will change again at 16 or 17. Parents, we need to help our kids set the right objectives as they grow up. The skills and values I highlight in this book are a great starting point.

That said, I encourage you to put grit on that list from *day one*. Unless you move to a country where people don't face difficulties, opposition, hardship, or failures in their pursuit of "something of value," your child will need grit.

This means that all "helicopter parents" who want to remove every obstacle from their kids' lives will need to leave the helicopter in the hangar. Stop micromanaging everything. Let go, at least a little. What would happen if we helped lift dumbbells for our kids? If we tried to lessen or remove the resistance required to challenge the muscles so they can grow larger and

Helping our children identify what they truly value is vital in fueling the engine to persevere through difficulties, to remain hopeful in spite of setbacks and failure.

stronger? The same principle applies to grit. Resistance facilitates growth. That's why resistance cannot be removed from the equation. There is a distinct difference and long-term impact with parents who intentionally prepare their kids to launch versus those who overly protect their kids before they launch. Either way they will be launched from your nest. Early in our parenting days, my wife and I committed to the former (prepare for launch), or as child development and behavior specialist Betsy Brown Braun states, "Prepare the child for the path, not the path for the child." The power of words is important when developing grit.[5] What you say, how you say it, and when you say it can build a kid up or tear her or him down. As parents, we can be firm *and* loving. We can encourage our kids to press on toward their objective as we highlight and commend their resolve, perseverance, and grit. We can push without tearing down. We can avoid negative, cutting words. We can help them understand that losing a game or match does not make someone a loser. And we can avoid embarrassing our kids in front of their teammates, coaches, opponents, and family members.

Remember that analogy from our "Self-Confidence" chapter: A $100-dollar bill that is wrinkled or caked with dirt is still worth 100 bucks. Its value is the same as a bill that just rolled off the press. Just brush off the dirt and smooth out the creases a bit, and you are good to go. So, when our kids are feeling damaged, we need to affirm their value.

Then we should seek to understand what blocked them from showing resilience or competing hard in a certain situation. That will help us determine the best course of action (more practice, role-playing, building self-confidence, fine-tuning technique, etc.) to better equip our kids to summon their courage the next time around.

Encouraging our kids to develop grit requires a "marathon mindset." Part of this mindset is understanding that a child's toughest opponent will be "the person in the mirror" (to quote Rocky Balboa). So, we need to slay that dragon of negative self-talk and use tools like personal affirmation daily to keep their cup full. "Me versus me" is a battle all kids face, so let's make sure our kids have great life coaches to help them in their journeys.

SUMMARY

1. Grit is the unyielding courage and continued effort to do or achieve something of value, in the face of difficulties, hardship, opposition, or failure.

2. Athletics provide the platform to develop grit as an athlete, but parents must uphold a similar standard to develop grit in a child's personal life.

3. Add grit to your child's scorecard. Qualities like this help a kid become a 5-star person who lives in his or her greatness.

4. Your words have power to build up or tear down your child as they develop grit. Help them identify, understand, and implement the best course of action to facilitate growth.

5. Combat negative self-talk. Encourage kids to speak words that align with positive self-talk and a growth mindset.

ACTIONABLE DEVELOPMENT

» Show them examples of gritty players in their sport on YouTube or other sites. Ask your son or daughter to identify and discuss what they see.

» Commend the specific times you see your young athlete displaying grit during practice or games. Ask, "How did that make you feel?" and "How were you able to push through those obstacles and be so resilient?" Then ask, "How can you apply that grit in your personal life—at home, school, and so on?"

>> Watch Angela Duckworth's 2013 Ted Talk on grit together. Then encourage your child to adopt Duckworth's "Hard Thing Rule." [4]

PERSONAL APPLICATION

Affirmation:

>> Affirm who they are, what they are capable of, and how much they matter on their grit journey.

Acknowledge:

>> The small acts of grit your child exemplifies as he or she conquers obstacles or unforeseen circumstances.

>> Acknowledge their hope and passion, or whatever motivates them to get back up and keep trying.

Reward:

>> Their strength of character to remain gritty even when conditions are tough and they are not expected to win (or even keep the score close). When your child is the underdog, assure him or her, "I *see* you."

19

A HEALTHY, ACTIVE LIFESTYLE

*"Never underestimate the value of good health.
Your health impacts every moment of your life."*

—ZERO DEAN [1]

TWO OF THE MOST valuable things in life cannot be bought: time and health. As they say in professional sports, "Father time is undefeated." Even the best athletes in the world will see their physical health wane and their abilities deteriorate. However, we have the ability to protect and enhance the quality of our health by the way we choose to live. Some people overlook one of the main benefits of youth sports: It encourages kids to develop a lifelong commitment to a healthy, active lifestyle. This lifestyle is a game changer on so many levels. It enhances a kid's physical, emotional, and mental health, both now and for a lifetime. What's more, many young athletes stay true to a healthy lifestyle even if they leave the world of competitive sports. They value being active and healthy, whether they are a member of the volleyball team or the marching band. Being healthy is a key to living in greatness. For kids to be the best version of themselves, they need to be healthy and active.

Let's look at some benefits of an active lifestyle, along with three recommended levels of physical activity (provided by the CDC).[2]

MENTAL AND EMOTIONAL HEALTH BENEFITS

» Improved thinking/cognitive skills

» Reduced risk of anxiety and depression

» Reduced stress levels

» Sharpened focus

» Improved academic performance. (High school student-athletes, for example, tend to earn higher grades and test scores than non-athletes.)

» Social development (Sports provide a feeling of belonging and acceptance among one's peers.)

» Improved self-esteem

PHYSICAL

» Improvements in muscle and bone growth

» Improved motor skills

» Improved balance

» Better-quality sleep

» Weight management (Young athletes enjoy a reduced risk of obesity.)

» Reduced risk of diseases, including cardiovascular ailments and diabetes.

RECOMMENDED ACTIVITY

1. **Aerobic Activity:** Most of your child's daily 60 minutes of physical activity should be aerobic activities like walking, running, or anything that raises the heart rate. Encourage your child to complement the aerobic work with at least three sessions of anaerobic activity—the things that make them breathe hard and get their hearts pumping vigorously.

2. **Muscle-Strengthening:** A child's daily 60 minutes of exercise should include at least three weekly sessions of muscle-strengthening activities, such as climbing, push-ups, or age-appropriate weightlifting.

3. **Bone-Strengthening:** Include bone-strengthening activities (such as jumping or running) at least three days per week.

Parents let's do our part by modeling healthy, active lifestyles. Let's make it a family priority. If your child sees you doing a workout video, doing yoga, going for a walk or bike ride, or shooting hoops in the driveway, he or she will see you live what you preach. And most kids value being part of a family that is active *together*. So, head to the park to hike or play softball. Play volleyball in the backyard or at the beach. Don't miss an opportunity to show the whole family what an active lifestyle looks like. Let's help our kids catch this vision and enjoy being active and healthy. For kids in highly competitive sports leagues like travel ball, club, or AAU, the importance of hydration, healthful and balanced meals, good snacks, sleeping eight hours for recovery, and extra stretching is paramount to being prepared, staying healthy and recovering properly. I remember forcing my "I'm invincible" children to drink a certain number of large water bottles daily during their competitive seasons. This continued until they understood the value for themselves (a few painful post-game cramps helped as well). Eventually, hydration became a habit to help them perform at their best, while reducing the risk of muscle injuries. Plus, they always saw me drink from my water bottle, which I also took to the office every day.

Remember, sports are not for everyone, but being healthy and active is. Regardless of age or ability, everyone can be active at some level. The key is to be consistent and make it fun. That way, our kids will want to be active, and they will make wise nutritional choices on their own. Getting them to take ownership of this lifestyle will take time, but the compounding interest and return on your investment will be well worth it.

SUMMARY

1. A healthy, active lifestyle affects your child's life mentally, emotionally, and physically.

2. The key to making healthy activity a lifestyle is to model it. So be consistent and make it fun.

3. Organized sports are not the only way to stay active. Commit to helping your child take ownership of good health, even when he or she is not competing in sports.

ACTIONABLE DEVELOPMENT

» Spend quality time with your child to uncover or remind them of their meaningful "why" in sports— what drives or excites them. Help them visualize and embrace it. Rinse and repeat this exercise when it comes to your child's academics and career aspirations.

» Encourage and give them permission to feel, to express emotions during triumphs and lessons learned during their young lives. This freedom will help their self-awareness blossom. Plus, when you listen with love and empathy, it will strengthen and enrich your bond with your child.

» Plan a weekly fun physical activity for your you and your child—or, better yet, for the whole family.

» Discover which physical activities your child enjoys most, and why.

» Strive to include more nutritional options in your child's snacks and meals. What can you do to "spice things up," in a healthful way?

» Discuss the importance of hydration before, during, and after physical activity. Let's involve our kids in the discussions and decisions about nutritional pre- and post-game meals.

PERSONAL APPLICATION

Affirmation:

» Affirm who they are, what they are capable of, and how much they matter on their healthy-and-active lifestyle journey.

» Affirm their progress and consistency.

Acknowledge:

» Their effort and self-discipline in making choice that are consistent with a healthy, active lifestyle

» Acknowledge that a healthy lifestyle is a journey, a process. Don't let anyone guilt-trip or body-shame your kid. (And don't let any kid do this to him- or herself.)

Reward:

» Find opportunities to celebrate effort, progress, and consistency.

20

THE KNACK (AND THE NOCK)
OF TEAMWORK

*"Teamwork is the ability to work together
toward a common vision. The ability to direct
individual accomplishments toward organizational
[team] objectives. It's the fuel that allows
common people attain uncommon results."*

—ANDREW CARNEGIE

I LOVE teamwork in sports! I thrive on seeing a team work together to accomplish a common goal. It's a beautiful sight when a team plays and operates as one, especially when you see it during breaks or after the game. There are so many valuable skills involved, activated, and developed through participation in team sports. Sports allow a young person to grow personally, gain experience in a variety of situations, and create conditions for personal success in life.

Teamwork includes agreeing on a common goal, communication, listening, empathy (seeing the other person's perspective), collaboration, accountability, responsibility, being trustworthy, problem-solving, critical thinking, camaraderie, love, respecting one another, commitment, inspiration, togetherness, joy, sadness, and, most importantly, RELATIONSHIP. All these elements and more are on display in competitive sports. Parenting your child to "live in greatness" means avoiding a "lone ranger" mentality. Rather, let's help our kids embrace the truth that greater significance can be accomplished together, rather than alone. Helen Keller's message is simple yet profound: "Alone we can do so little. Together we can do so much." [2] Sports provide the perfect setting to develop and reinforce teamwork. Athletics create seeds for parents to plant and water in the garden of each child's personal life, starting at home.

Teamwork reflects humankind's innate need for relationship, to connect with others. In the beginning, there was only one thing created that was not deemed "good": being alone. Our world is constructed and built upon that relational need, in how we live, work, and play together. I believe sports is the greatest teacher of teamwork. It helps a kid learn that achieving anything significant will require working with others at some point.

Basketball provides a clear example of teamwork. (Of course, softball, soccer, football, baseball, hockey, lacrosse, volleyball, and so on all have similar elements of teamwork, although they are sometimes expressed differently due to each sport's framework.) In basketball, when a shot is taken, team members box out opposing players. Once a rebound is secured, the rebounder throws an outlet pass to a guard. The guard passes the ball to a streaking forward, who can take a shot. Let's look at all the lessons we can learn from this simple series of events:

Responsibility: Getting a rebound is a shared goal. The players who don't secure the rebound are accountable to box out opposing players. That clears the way for a teammate to grab the rebound.

Communication: Established through hours of practice, communication helps players understand their roles. A forward or center who grabs a rebound knows that the next step is to pass the ball to a guard, a skilled ball handler who can lead a fast break. On the court, a guard often calls for the ball, letting the rebounder know where he is.

Commitment: The players commit to boxing out and ensuring their team gets the rebound. Then, the team members fill specific lanes as they sprint down the floor on a fast break. If even one person fails to "run the break," the team's scoring options are reduced, and the opposing team can double-team the guard, making harder for him to pass the ball.

Trust and dependability: Basketball players must continually trust one another. The rebounder trusts that his teammates will box out. The guard trusts that he is going to get the ball so he can lead the break. And all of the players trust each other as they work together to run the court and (often) make multiple passes to ensure that the player who ultimately shoots has *the best possible shot*. (Dependable basketball players often give up a *good* shot for themselves, passing the ball so that one of their teammates gets a *great* shot.)

Taking that shot requires critical thinking: ("Do I pull up for a jump shot or move around the defender for a layup?") When the shot is made, it's an individual contribution to the *team* score. The whole team (briefly) celebrates a successful fast break, knowing that all five people on the floor contributed to the success.

Then, everyone runs back down the court to set up on defense, ready for more problem-solving—to prevent the other team from scoring.

Poise under pressure: All of this happens with a bunch of people watching, often including a player's family, friends, and classmates. (And the fans of the opposing team as well.)

Consistency: Hours of game and practice time allow a team to run the break fluidly and dependably.

I hope the example above helps you appreciate all of the mental and physical elements of teamwork and character repeatedly being forged into young people, play after play. Yes, those young athletes are having fun, but they are also investing thousands of hours into mastering their skills. Imagine what can happen if they apply the same discipline in other areas of life, such as their studies and, ultimately, their careers and personal lives?

The Warrior Parent Mentality affirms and celebrates the value of team and the importance of each individual's role in team success. We celebrate the personal connections, the support of one another, the sense of personal responsibility, the sacrifices, the communication, and all of the other elements that contribute to the beauty of functioning as a team. These qualities will accelerate growth in your child, regardless of his or her role on the team. As Phil Jackson, the 11-time NBA championship coach stated, "The

A win (whether it's on the court or in the backyard) is that much sweeter when everyone plays a part.

strength of the team is each individual member; the strength of each member is the team." (Jackson, by the way, also won two championship rings as a player. He was a defensive specialist for the New York Knicks.) [3]

Don't let social media, personal ego, or statistics define anyone's worth to his or her team. Phil Jackson coached legends like Michael Jordan and Kobe Bryant. He convinced them of the importance of each team member, from the all-stars to the guys at the end of the bench, who saw most of their action during practice. Jordan reflected his coach's philosophy when he said, "Talent wins games, but teamwork and intelligence wins *championships*." [4]

As Warrior Parents, we are committed to raising champions in life. Period!

How can you activate and empower your child to thrive on teamwork? First, model it at home. For example, a "Guidry Man" must know how to BBQ. It's a family rite of passage, so we "Q" often at our Southern California home. I love making BBQ a family affair and cultivating teamwork. When our family sits down to enjoy the meal together, I make sure that everyone has contributed. A win (whether it's on the court or in the backyard) is that much sweeter when everyone plays a part.

I do "the Q'ing." My wife and daughter prepare the side dishes. The boys are responsible for setting the table and pouring the drinks. And, of course, they must listen to Dad as he shares the Guidry BBQ skills with the next generation. The kids vie for the privilege of controlling the music—until my wife steps in and throws on the soulful playlist, featuring Steve Wonder, Chaka Khan, and Earth, Wind, and Fire (so that we can dance a bit and teach the kids about *real* music!) After all, teamwork is supposed to be fun. The journey toward the vision should be enjoyed. Once everything is ready, we sit at the table together and say grace. We want to teach the kids gratitude for the provision and the hands who prepared it. (And remember, everybody helped in the preparation.)

We intentionally combat entitlement, which is such a plague in today's society. That's one reason that clean-up is a team effort as well, with Mom and Dad doing the least and the older kids doing the most. That's your simple example of teamwork in the Guidry household. I encourage you to adopt something similar when it comes to family dinners, daily chores, or any activity based on shared objectives.

Parents don't fall into the trap of limiting your child by failing to provide the opportunity to work and contribute to family activities. There will be class projects, sports, and other extracurricular activities. There will be part-time jobs, and, one day, a career. All of these will include the need to work together as a team. Your kids will face pressure to perform. That's why it is important to build confidence and discipline right now. Remember, you are crafting arrows that will soar in life. And life is not a solo event. As the African proverb reminds us, "If you want to go fast, go alone. If you want to go far, go together."

SUMMARY

1. Teamwork is the ability to work together toward a common vision.

2. We are built to be relational beings. Learning teamwork is vital in your child's personal development, whatever his or her life goals might be.

3. Anything of significance is achieved through the cooperation, support, or teamwork of others.

ACTIONABLE DEVELOPMENT

» Pick a family activity that includes teamwork and use it as a teaching tool. Share the role of leader, as well as all of the roles involved.

» Model and share how you use teamwork in your job and important personal endeavors, such as pursuing an advanced degree or planning a holiday family gathering.

» Watch sports movies or action-hero movies and discuss how teamwork leads to achieving goals. Ask your kids to identify the personal qualities that they admire or identify with.

» Find video clips that highlight teamwork in a kid's favorite sport. (YouTube is a great source for these.) Kids should be able to see teamwork in action, appreciating the beauty of everyone working together.

PERSONAL APPLICATION

Affirm:

» Affirm who your kids are, what they are capable of, and how much they matter, as they exemplify teamwork in practice and games, in school and at home.

» Let your daughter or son know you love watching them play, whether it's in a game, shooting baskets in the driveway, or playing catch in the backyard.

Acknowledge:

» Make sure to highlight their growth as a member of a team. Point out specific qualities, such as communication, unselfishness, trust, camaraderie, encouragement, and so on.

» Identify how their individual contribution helped the team toward a win, or even success during a specific play. This is a great way to reinforce the truth that every member of the team is important, and every role is important.

Reward:

» Celebrate a kid's teamwork with a treat after a game, or after a morning of doing chores. Make teamwork something to enjoy and celebrate.

21

FAITH
(THE BONUS LIFE SKILL)

"Faith by itself isn't enough.
Unless it produces good deeds,
it is dead and useless."

—JAMES 2:17 (NLT)

IF THERE WAS a Faith Hall of Fame, it would have
to include Noah, who built a massive ark in preparation for a
massive flood that was years away from happening. And how
about Sarah, who held fast to God's promise that she would
bear a child—even though she was 90 years old. And then there
was Daniel, who bravely faced the lions' den and emerged
unharmed.

In sports, the accomplishments are not of biblical propor-
tions. However, many athletes have an active faith in God (or
higher power), something they hope for but can't see.

In 2015, for example, my son Javelin (then a sophomore) finished last in the finals of the Texas 5A 100-meter dash. After the race, my wife and I congratulated him and expressed how proud we were.

But before we left the stadium, I asked him "Where do you see yourself finishing next track season?"

He replied, "On the medal podium." He spoke his faith. He activated it.

> For many of us, faith is an integral part of our lives. It's not just an emergency solution for disasters or circumstances beyond our control. I believe that faith in a higher power is an important part of helping a child develop as a person and live in greatness daily.

After his 11th grade football season (which culminated with winning the 5A Texas State Championship), Javelin decided not to play basketball. This was a conscious sacrifice he made, in pursuit of his "faith podium goal." He spent the three winter months of basketball season putting in extra work to prepare for track in the spring. He made sure his actions were in line with his faith.

How did that work out? He didn't merely get on the podium after the 100-meter 5A Texas state finals; he won the gold medal. In fact, he didn't lose a 100-meter race all season long.

Fast-forward to his senior year in high school (which included a move from Texas to California). This time, he applied his faith toward the goal of being the 100-meter state champ in California—and becoming the first athlete to win that race in both states.

He accomplished his goal, with a blazing 10.13w, setting a new state record.[1] His faith in God, his abilities, and his work ethic inspired my wife and me to believe that an ordinary young athlete can achieve the extraordinary—if he or she has faith.

Many athletes (and sometimes whole teams) recognize that having faith in something greater than oneself can serve as a great source of motivation and purpose. Some athletes incorporate their faith into their sport by acknowledging God or a higher power as the source of their abilities. They thank God for opportunities, they rely on him when battling injury, and they strive to follow him in the way they live.

You have probably seen teams pray together before or after a game. And you may have seen players take a knee in prayer during a game, after a touchdown, or when a teammate or an opponent suffers a serious injury.

For many of us, faith is an integral part of our lives. It's not just an emergency solution for disasters or circumstances beyond our control. I believe that faith in a higher power is an important part of helping a child develop as a person and live in greatness daily. I like how UCLA's legendary Coach John Wooden explained it: "There are many things that are essential to arriving at true peace of mind, and one of the most important is faith, which cannot be acquired without prayer."[2]

Some of sports' brightest athletes have shared how faith influences their lives, within and beyond sports. Here are just a few of the solid role models who live out their faith and give our kids people to look up to: NBA Champion Stephen Curry, Clemson's national champ QB Trevor Lawrence, WNBA champion Maya Moore, Super-Bowl winning QB Russell Wilson, and USA Women's Gymnastics gold medal winner Gabby Douglas.

SUMMARY

1. Faith is the confidence in things hoped for and the assurance of what we do not see.

2. Faith is activated and exercised in sports.

3. Faith in oneself (and in a power *greater* than oneself) is an important part of PERSONal development and living in greatness.

ACTIONABLE DEVELOPMENT

» Help your child understand what they believe and be able to defend it. (In other words, "What do you believe, and why do you believe it?")

» Encourage your child to incorporate faith into everyday life, in sports and beyond. Discuss how faith should affect the way we speak, the way we compete, and how we treat others (including coaches, teammates, opponents, and officials).

» Encourage them to memorize Bible verses (or passages from other faith traditions).

PERSONAL APPLICATION

Affirmation:

> » Let's affirm what God (or your higher power) says about who your kids are, what they are capable of, and how much they matter.

Acknowledge:

> » Let's ask our kids, "What parts of your life align with your faith? What might be out of alignment?"

> » Practice gratitude daily. Encourage kids to acknowledge all the good things they have in life.

> » How can you model faith? Encouraging is good, but showing is better. Say a prayer of thanks before meals. Pray for people in need. Encourage your kids to be generous with their time, money, and other resources. Participate in charitable efforts sponsored by your church or other faith-based organization.

Reward:

> » Celebrate when they put actions toward their faith in the little things!

EPILOGUE

LAUNCHING ARROWS

2016. 2017. 2018. 2019. These are the consecutive years in which my wife (Dr. MamaKai) and our three children (Javelin, Elisha, and Kailah Grace) graduated from medical school and high school, respectively. My wife was launched into a medical residency program, while my kids headed for college.

During this time, the concept of "being launched" was discussed frequently. We ingrained in our kids the expectation that, after high school, you continue to learn and grow. You attend college, or you attend a trade school to develop a skill. Maybe you jump right into the workforce and become an entrepreneur. Whichever target they chose, the trajectory was going to be high.

However, I don't want to offer some photo-shopped, social-media-friendly version of our launching stories. Just as a skilled archer trains, practices, prepares, and studies to master his craft, my wife and I had to sacrifice, work hard, and hone our skills.

No one saw all that we endured as young parents (21 and 23), to get to where we are today. The desperate prayers while living on WIC, the stress that caused breaking out in hives, the 120-mile work commutes, the time and expense of extra training sessions, the F's on report cards, the late nights and early mornings spent on homework and test preparation, the counseling sessions, and the issues with in-laws.

Then there were the challenges brought on by relocating for medical school three times in four years, moving thousands of miles from one home to the next during our kids' adolescent years.

Ultimately, our faith sustained us. We were real with each other, and we stuck together. By practicing the life skills I share in this book, we enabled our kids to successfully launch. Today, we are confident in each kid's personal development. We know they will thrive and live in their own greatness.

There were so many lessons we learned as we launched our children. It would require another book, written with Dr. MamaKai, to effectively convey our family's secret sauce. However, I will share the following basic principles, which I encourage you to apply to your child's life before he or she completes high school, with hopes it will follow them into adult life. After all, parenting doesn't stop with graduation.

» Encourage them to dream, imagine, and WRITE OUT their vision.

» Include faith in God (or other higher power) throughout the process.

» Set "stretch goals"—targets one can hit on the journey to the ultimate goal.

» Give them freedom to fail, and encourage them to learn from each failure.

» Create a culture of personal growth, excellence, and greatness at home

» Provide exposure to people, careers, and experiences that will inspire them and help them see what's possible.

» Be a *parent*. Be loving, be firm, be consistent, be adaptable, be a good listener, and be intentional.

» Walk in Presence, Power and Purpose (WP3). Live in the moment!!!

WP3 SPORTS IS...

Live in Greatness

A CALL TO ACTION! A call to create a new normal and the highest version of youth and high school sports. WP3 Sports equips parents, coaches, leagues, and schools in the holistic character development of young people, regardless of talent level. It's a commitment to personally enable young people to live in greatness, both on the court or field and beyond. It's the post-pandemic rainbow that shifts the paradigm of sports programs as it prepares and enables young people to apply sports-related skills and disciplines (honed for dozens of hours) to all aspects of their personal life! Ultimately, WP3 is an empowerment program to develop life skills and unleash all the greatness that lies in each young person. It's the practical application or implementation plan for the *Warrior Parent Playbook* with teammates.

The Mission and Vision of WP3 Sports are clear:

Mission: Equip, Empower, and Inspire young people to Live in Greatness every day.

Vision: To enable parents, coaches, and administrators to utilize sports for holistic character and life skills development of young people. To shape and prepare young people to launch into the world.

WP3 Sports provides multiple individual and team-based character and life skills development programs for young people ages 8-19—including a sports social community-based application that encourages positive actions to make kids better athletes and people, who give back to the community. Some of the core pillars of the programs include:

» Parent-child daily interaction (10+ minutes a day) focused on life skill development and personal application in all aspects of life during their sports season.

» An enriching team or community-based participation structure in a fun social environment.

» Mobile/Web application providing relevant digital content, growth resources, fun gamification activities, and positive action-based engagement for the athlete, parent, and coach.

PARTNERSHIP

WP3 Sports is partnering with leagues, schools, and parents who want to invest in their children's character development through sports. They will apply the knowledge shared in this book and will commit to adapting and integrating it to this new way of doing sports. The WP3 Live in Greatness application provides a relevant digital platform to facilitate the life skills program and creates a fun, innovative way to encourage positive actions in building the next generation of high-character leaders.

There will be bumps along the way: life adjustments and some discomfort. But remember, "Growth and comfort cannot co-exist." What's better, you won't be alone on this path; the program is designed to be a part of a team or community of like-minded, imperfect people, all striving toward developing young people from the inside out. My WP3 Sports team is committed to supporting you along the way with empathy and care.

Let me be clear: WP3 Sports is not a guarantee or magic bullet to make your child super successful in school or athletics or in their future career. It is not designed to tell a coach how to handle your child. (However, I believe many coaches will integrate WP3 Sports' principles into their coaching regimen.)

It is not designed to tell you exactly how to parent your child. Each household and young person is different. However, I am confident that the *Warrior Parent Playbook* offers treasures of enriching principles and information. WP3 Sports will help optimize the value of sports, for you and your child.

Lastly, it is my prayer and deepest desire that individual lives will be transformed, families positively impacted, and, one day at a time, your child will joyfully and confidently embrace the call to "live in their greatness." My fellow parents, we must own the fact that we are all works in progress. We are running the marathon called life together. But every day we all have the opportunity to express the best and fullest version of ourselves. That, my friends, is your greatness!

WWW.WP3SPORTS.COM

WP3sports | @WP3sports | @WP3sports

info@wp3sports.com

schools@wp3sports.com

leagues@wp3sports.com

ACKNOWLEDGMENTS

FAITH, FAMILY, SPORTS, and Coaching are the core pillars in my life. They make my world come alive. This book is a passionate expression of my journey and a testament of God's grace at work throughout my life. Its inspiration came from God. However, there are many people who also contributed to bringing these words to life, through countless experiences and immeasurable acts of enduring love.

I must begin by acknowledging my Lord and Savior, Jesus Christ, whose unconditional love and matchless grace sees past my brokenness to unlock the greatness inside of me—for the world to experience. Through his love, I hope to spread love to others through these pages to help make parents, children, and families a little bit better.

To my beautiful wife, Kaishauna, and amazing children, Javelin K., Elisha, and Kailah: Thank you for your love and support throughout this process. Thank you for listening to me share stories and insights over and over and over again. We make a great team and are truly blessed!

Thank you to my hero and father, Edward "Ace" Guidry. Your love, commitment to family, and example of coaching people "showed me the way" like only you could. I am evidence that you were here, and your Guidry legacy lives on. I miss you, Dad!

To my mom, Brenda Guidry, and brother, Paul Guidry: Thank you for supporting me and encouraging me to share all of myself with the world.

Thanks to my college mentor and couples coach, Rod Hairston. My family and I are honored to call Rod and his lovely bride, Sheri, friends. Thank you, Rod and Sheri, for helping us see intentional parenting firsthand.

To all my coaches, fellow coaches, team moms, parents, and the former players I've coached throughout the years: THANK YOU! You played a part in making this book happen. Let's celebrate this together!

To my editor, Todd Hafer, and graphic designer, Peter Gloege, thank you for helping make my first book become professional and sharp. I think it's ready for prime time!

I am grateful to all the athletes referenced in this book—and so many more. Thank you for sharing your gifts with the world and inspiring so many. I hope to do my part by utilizing sports to empower and equip parents to raise and launch children to be the next generation of high-character leaders who will make this world a better place by unleashing their greatness.

To my best friend, Demetrius Nathan Roaché "Jimbo", whom we lost too soon. You were the reason I wore jersey number 3, and your number will live on in WP3 Sports. I made our dreams a reality and so much more. . . .

Finally, I'd be remiss if I didn't acknowledge two individuals, we lost in 2020 who impacted millions of lives globally: Kobe Bryant, "The Black Mamba," and Chadwick Boseman, "The Black Panther." Their lives and character inspired and gave hope to me and so many people. They showed us how to be the best version of ourselves—and demonstrated that a super-hero can be black and make the entire world a better place. "The Mamba Mentality" and "Wakanda Forever" are slogans from two transcendent generational figures. More importantly, they represent mindsets that will transform lives forever. Kobe's and Chadwick's impact and influence awakened and inspired one of my book's major themes: "Live in Greatness!" I am thankful to have witnessed and learned from these great men!

Gratefully,
Your friend, Coach Jav!

NOTES

Prologue

1. https://www.businesswire.com/news/home/20190514005472/en/Sports and https://fortune.com/fortune500/2018/.

2. For a great summary of the benefits of youth sports, see https://www.aspenprojectplay.org/youth-sports-facts.

3. For more information on Little League Baseball, see https://www.littleleague.org/play-little-league/league-finder.

4. https://www.aspenprojectplay.org/youth-sports-facts.

Chapter One

1. https://en.wikiquote.org/wiki/Ursula_K._Le_Guin. This quote is from Le Guin's book *The Left Hand of Darkness*.

2. Among those who have made similar statements to Uncle Ben's famous Spider-Man quote: Jesus Christ, Lord Melbourne, Winston Churchill, Teddy Roosevelt, and Franklin D. Roosevelt. See quoteinvestigator.com/2015/07/23/great-power/.

3. https://www.biography.com/athlete/arthur-ashe.

Chapter Two

1. For more information on Rachel Garcia's accomplishments, see https://uclabruins.com/sports/softball/roster/rachel-garcia/9852.

2. For more information on LeBron James the businessman, see https://www.one37pm.com/strength/sports/lebron-net-worth.

Chapter Three

1. This John Maxwell quote is from a 2017 speech. See https://umobile.edu/news/university-mobile-scholarship-speaker-john-maxwell-urges-life-significance/).

2. Muhammad Ali's name was still Cassius Clay when he fought Liston. He changed his name shortly after the fight. For more of Ali's famous quotes, see https://www.abc.net.au/news/2016-06-04/muhammad-ali-greatest-quotes.

3. The phrase "Often imitated, never duplicated" was a slogan of Traub Manufacturing Company, a Detroit-based firm that was famous in the early 1900s for its Orange Blossom line of engagement rings and wedding bands.

4. For more information on Maya Angelou, see (https://www.biographbook.com/maya-angelous-coming-of-age-life-story/).

5. Beyonce's daughter Blue Ivy Carter helped write the song "Brown Skin Girl" and also contributed vocals. See https://www.songfacts.com/facts/beyonce/brown-skin-girl.

6. See "Practice Six" of *The Sudden Loss Survival Guide* by Chelsea Hanson. (Mango Publishing, 2020).

Chapter Four

1. This quote is from Jon Gordon's Twitter: https://twitter.com/jongordon11/status/1067233948638617600?lang=en.

2. Women are now allowed in the Navy SEALs. (https://www.npr.org/sections/thetwo-way/2017/07/20/538338758/the-navy-gets-its-first-female-seal-candidate).

3. The "21 days to form a habit" concept was introduced in a 1960 self-help book by cosmetic surgeon Dr. Maxwell Maltz, titled *Psycho Cybernetics, A New Way to Get More Living Out of Life* (Prentice Hall Press).

4. This quote is from Brendon Burchard's book *The Motivation Manifesto* (Hay House, 2014, page 76).

5. http://www.quoteswise.com/john-wooden-quotes-4.html.

Chapter Five

1. For more Michael Jordan stats, see https://www.basketball-reference.com/players/j/jordami01.html.

2. https://www.milb.com/birmingham/news/tim-anderson-wins-mlb-al-batting-title-310971796.

3. This book went to press before the 2019-2020 NBA season was complete. https://www.basketball-reference.com/players/h/hillge01.html.

4. https://www.successories.com/iquote/author/30220/tom-bradley-quotes/1.

5. Translations abound for this famous quote from Laozi (in the *Tao Te Ching*, chapter 64, line 12). See https://en.wikiquote.org/wiki/Laozi.

Chapter Six

1. This quote is from Paulo Coelho classic *The Alchemist*. See also: https://en.wikiquote.org/wiki/Paulo_Coelho.

2. Michael Phelps has won 28 total Olympic medals, 23 of them gold. For more information, see https://www.olympicchannel.com/en/athletes/detail/michael-phelps-ii/.

3. https://www.oprah.com/spirit/what-oprah-knows-for-sure-about-lifes-biggest-adventure.

4. https://www.belfasttelegraph.co.uk/sport/football/premier-league/claudio-ranieri-interview-what-he-said-34683065.html.

5. This Wintley Phipps quote is often attributed to Oprah Winfrey, despite her efforts to credit Phipps. (https://www.oprah.com/omagazine/what-oprah-knows-for-sure-about-finding-success).

Chapter Seven

1. https://eastonarchery.com/2014/01/nocks-the-vital-connection/.

Chapter Eight

1. For more information on Sequoia trees, see https://www.mentalfloss.com/article/92177/10-towering-facts-about-giant-sequoias.

2. https://behindtheathlete.es/en/blog/legacy-eng.

3. This Rick Warren quote, from page 53 of his book *The Purpose Driven Life* (Zondervan), is often misattributed to C.S. Lewis. See https://en.wikiquote.org/wiki/Rick_Warren.

4. For more on the science of gratitude, see https://health.ucdavis.edu/medicalcenter/features/2015-2016/11/20151125_gratitude.html.

5. http://coachjohnwoodenquotes.blogspot.com/2011/01/ability-may-get-you-to-top-but-it-takes.html.

Chapter Nine

1. https://www.teamusa.org/USA-Field-Hockey/Features/2019/April/03/Hard-Work-Beats-Talent-When-Talent-Doesnt-Work-Hard.

2. In 2017, *Sports Illustrated* named J.J. Watt its Sportsperson of the Year. See also, https://247sports.com/Player/5236/Quotes/Greatness-is-earned-not-given-35896366/.

Chapter Ten

1. For more information on the connection between youth-sports participation and business success, see https://www.coachup.com/nation/articles/95-of-fortune-500-ceos-were-athletes.

2. Ginni Rometty, current Executive Chairman of IBM, stepped aside from her role as the firm's CEO in early 2020. See https://beleaderly.com/leaderly-quote-i-learned-to-always/.

Chapter Eleven

1. This quote is from Henley's 1875 poem "I Am the Master of My Fate."

2. https://melrobbins.com/key-real-confidence-daily-acts-everyday-courage/.

3. For more information on the financial struggles of former pro athletes, see https://www.investopedia.com/financial-edge/0312/why-athletes-go-broke.

4. This quote is from the book *Burn Your Goals* by Joshua Medcalf and Jamie Gilbert (Lulu Publishing Services, 2015).

5. Brian Tracy, *The Power of Self-Confidence* (Hoboken, NJ: John Wiley & Sons, Inc., 2012), 3.

Chapter Twelve

1. https://theconversation.com/how-maya-angelou-made-me-feel-27328.

2. https://www.inc.com/peter-economy/44-inspiring-john-c-maxwell-quote.

3. https://www.linkedin.com/pulse/20-favorite-quotes-from-extreme-ownership. See also: https://boxpromag.com/what-is-extreme-ownership/.

4. For more information on great quarterbacks and great comebacks, see https://www.pro-football-reference.com/leaders/comebacks_career.htm.

5. https://www.workforgood.org/article/advancing-your-personal-leadership-one-step-at-a-time. See also: https://twitter.com/johncmaxwell/status/967069491686494209?lang=en.

Chapter Thirteen

1. For more information on Kobe Bryant and the 2008 "Redeem Team," see https://bleacherreport.com/articles/2795121-how-kobe-bryant-led-the-rebirth-of-usa-basketball.

2. https://www.thehopefullinstitute.com/wp-content/uploads/2020/02/THI-BookSummary-04-Legacy.pdf.

Chapter Fourteen

1. https://www.inc.com/dave-kerpen/15-quotes-on-passion-to-inspire-a-better-life.html.

2. https://www.forbes.com/sites/danschawbel/2017/01/09/angela-duckworth-a-passion-is-developed-more-than-it-is-discovered/#250c54023c0b.

Chapter Fifteen

1. https://www.successconsciousness.com/blog/inner-strength/what-is-self-discipline/.

2. Excerpted from the book *The Mamba Mentality: How I Play* by Kobe Bryant (illustrated edition published in 2018 by MCD).

3. https://www.goodreads.com/work/quotes/22300682-the-one-thing-the-surprisingly-simple-truth-behind-extraordinary-results.

4. This sobering statistic is from the National Alliance for Youth Sports. For more information, see https://www.washingtonpost.com/news/parenting/wp/2016/06/01/why-70-percent-of-kids-quit-sports-by-age-13/.

Chapter Sixteen

1. Australian rower Bo Hanson won three Olympic medals. He is now a coaching consultant and corporate trainer. See https://www.athleteassessments.com/do-you-have-adaptability-in-sport/ and https://www.rise-athletes.com/rise-blog/adaptability.

2. For more on Myron Rolle, see https://www.cnbc.com/2020/04/09/myron-rolle-nfl-player-turned-doctor-on-covid-19-front-line.html.

3. https://gantdaily.com/2017/05/19/myron-rolles-journey-from-nfl-to-neurosurgery/.

4. https://www.okcu.edu/news/women-in-leadership-conference-to-feature-communications-expert/.

Chapter Eighteen

1. Angela Duckworth, Grit: The Power of Passion and Perseverance (New York, NY: Scribner, an imprint of Simon & Schuster, 2016), xv.

2. For more information on the great (and gritty) Simone Biles, see https://www.biography.com/athlete/simone-biles#:~:text.

3. https://blogs.scientificamerican.com/beautiful-minds/grit-bringing-passion-back/.

4. The four elements of the Duckworth family's "Hard Thing Rule" are:
a. Everyone has to do a hard thing. b. You can quit, but not any time. c. You get to pick your hard thing. d. You must commit to your "hard thing" for at least two years. For more information, see https://www.thegameoffew.com/blog/2017/3/12/the-hard-thing-rule.

5. https://betsybrownbraun.com/betsyisms/betsys-favorite-things/

Chapter Nineteen

1. Zero Dean is an author, photographer, and filmmaker. For more information, see https://zerodean.com/content/never-underestimate-the-value-of-good-health/.

2. For more information on the CDC's recommended activity levels, see https://www.cdc.gov/physicalactivity/basics/children/index.htm#.

Chapter Twenty

1. This Andrew Carnegie quote is often misattributed to Dale Carnegie. The two were not related. See https://www.wiseoldsayings.com/authors/andrew-carnegie-quotes/.

2. This quote from Helen Keller is often misattributed to Mother Teresa.

3. No one in NBA history has matched Phil Jackson's 13 total NBA championships. See https://sports.yahoo.com/phil-jackson-gladly-show-13-nba-championship-rings.

4. Michael Jordan, *I Can't Accept Not Trying* (San Francisco, CA: HarperSanFrancisco, 1994), 20.

Chapter Twenty-One

1. Javelin Guidry Jr.'s 10.13 is the fastest all-conditions time in California prep history. It is not the official state record, due to a slightly higher than allowable tailwind. Javelin also ran a 4.29 40-yard dash at the 2020 NFL Combine. See https://arizonasports.com/story/2279617/utah-cb-javelin-guidry-runs-a-4-29-40-yard-dash-at-nfl-combine/.

2. https://www.thewoodeneffect.com/motivational-quotes.

JAVELIN M. GUIDRY is the author of the *Warrior Parent Playbook* and founder of the WP3 Sports life-skills-development program for young athletes and their parents. He grew up in Cerritos, CA, playing a variety of youth sports, including soccer for the Cerritos United, football in Orange County's Junior All American program, and Slam-N-Jam AAU basketball. A multi-sport star at Gahr High School in Cerritos, Javelin earned a full football scholarship to UCLA, where he was a three-year starter at cornerback.

As a Bruin, Javelin played in the defensive backfield with his brother, Paul. He ended his collegiate career as team captain. Today, he shares his gridiron knowledge at Vista Murrieta High School, where he has coached varsity football for the past two years.

He has been married to his college sweetheart, Kaishauna Guidry, MD, for 23 years. They have three amazing children, whom Javelin coached in youth sports in Southern California and Texas. Sons Javelin K. and Elisha led their teams to youth football championships and, later, high school state championships in Texas and California. Javelin K. holds California's state record in the 100-meter dash, at 10.13w seconds. Both sons earned full football scholarships (Javelin K. at the University of Utah and Elisha at UCLA). Currently, Elisha is a junior honor roll student athlete at UCLA and Javelin K. is a new member of the NFL's New York Jets. Daughter Kailah is a sophomore honor roll pre-med student at San Diego State University.

Prior to launching WP3 Sports, Javelin worked as an IT business professional and entrepreneur for 19 years. In addition to coaching football, he served as team chaplain for the Los Angeles Avengers of the Arena Football League and provided personal training in speed, agility, and football skills.

The *Warrior Parent Playbook* reflects the author's four core life pillars: faith, family, sports, and coaching. In his free time, Javelin enjoys outdoor activities, BBQing with family, and traveling to explore the world.

CPSIA information can be obtained
at www.ICGtesting.com
Printed in the USA
LVHW051507171220
674417LV00005B/733

9 781735 931401